MISSING
STORIES
of the
New Testament

David A. deSilva, PhD

Victor H. Matthews, PhD

Publications International, Ltd.

Author: David A. deSilva, PhD, is a Trustees' Distinguished Professor of Biblical Studies at Ashland Theological Seminary (Ohio). He has written several books including *4 Maccabees, Honor Discourse and the New Testament,* and *Praying with John Wesley.* In addition, he has published numerous articles and contributed to the *Dictionary of the Later New Testament* and *Dictionary of New Testament Backgrounds.*

Author: Victor H. Matthews, PhD, is a professor of Religious Studies at Missouri State University. His publication list includes *The Old Testament: Text and Context* and *Old Testament Parallels: Stories and Laws from the Ancient Near East.* He contributed numerous articles to the *Anchor Bible Dictionary,* and his writing often appears in *The Bible Today, Biblical Theology Bulletin,* and *Biblical Archaeologist.*

Louis Weber, CEO
Publications International, Ltd.
8140 Lehigh Avenue
Morton Grove, Illinois 60053

Permission is never granted for commercial purposes.

ISBN-13: 978-1-4508-7322-2
ISBN-10: 1-4508-7322-7

Manufactured in China.

8 7 6 5 4 3 2 1

Contents

Expanding Our Understanding
of the New Testament...................................4

Mary and Joseph 9

Stories of Jesus' Infancy 25

Stories of Jesus' Ministry 36

Jesus' Trial, Death,
and Resurrection 49

Peter, the Apostle
of Jesus..74

The Apostle Andrew 96

John the Apostle 107

Paul, Apostle to the Gentiles................ 117

Expanding Our Understanding of the New Testament

ave you ever thought about what Jesus might have been like as a child, what his father thought about him in later life, or what became of apostles like Peter, John, and Paul? If you have, you are not alone. Christians know what the Bible says about these figures, but many have longed to gain a deeper glimpse, to know more than biblical pages reveal. Over the centuries, a multitude of legends developed to fill in gaps in the Bible's stories. Some explain troubling details in the Bible, while others use a biblical story as a starting point for a new revelation or moral exhortation. Still others simply provide more information about those interesting figures about whom people wish the Bible said more.

This book will introduce you to many stories about figures from the New Testament—some whose names will be familiar and others who will be unfamiliar. These stories were told during the first few centuries after Jesus and his apostles lived. They arc not presented here as "true" in the sense of preserving accurate information about historical events. It is unlikely that any of the stories presented here actually happened, but they *do* tell us something valuable about the way in which early Christians read their scriptures and shared their stories. They also reveal how the early church may have dealt with problems they perceived in the biblical stories. These stories can teach us today about how early Christians derived and passed on moral instruction, as well as how they built their sense of identity in the midst of a world dominated by nonbelievers. Traditions and legends about Jesus—and the activities of his inner circle of apostles—also tell us something about the interest of the early church in its founders.

Missing Stories of the New Testament offers some possibilities to illuminate what we know about Jesus, his family, and his disciples. Early Christian writers from the second to fifth centuries A.D. filled

in many gaps in the story of Jesus. These traditions focused particularly on his youth (the "lost
years") and on the three days between his death
and resurrection. A number of these works focus
on the experience of Mary or Joseph, showing the
early church's interest in the lives of these specially

favored parents
and, in some
cases, their rela-
tionship to their
extraordinary son.
Some of these
writings became
very popular,
evidenced by the
number of copies

Jesus and his disciples

of ancient manuscripts that have survived. Many,
however, served the needs and suited the sensibili-
ties of only a small segment of the church.

Another group of writings, using the New
Testament "Acts of the Apostles" as their model, fill
out the details of the missionary activities and, in
many cases, the martyrdoms of the apostles. Some

of these, such as the *Acts of Paul,* the *Acts of Andrew,* the *Acts of John,* and the *Acts of Peter,* appear to have been available in written form as early as the third century A.D. While a number of them were rejected as heretical and unreliable by the main body of the church, a few were esteemed for a time as literature that could strengthen the faith and commitment of its readers.

Once again, these stories do *not* preserve what can be called reliable historical information, except perhaps in the barest sense (the fact that Paul and Peter were martyred in Rome, for example). Instead, the traditions tell us much more about what some early Christians thought about their founders, about what they wanted to believe concerning the lives and deaths of their apostles. Many stories had a moral lesson that would have been valued in the early centuries of the church, such as the defeat of magic before the true power of God as seen in Simon the Sorcerer's fate. Tales of the martyrdoms of the apostles may have been circulated to encourage Christians facing fiery waves of persecution in the middle- to late-third century

A.D. (though these traditions are also frequently regarded as preserving some reliable historical information).

This book, then, offers a collection of tradition and legend about figures known from the pages of the New Testament. In the absence of reliable history, it is, ultimately, all we have. These traditions bear witness to the ongoing, vital interaction between Christian believer and sacred text— sometimes rewriting, sometimes expanding, but always returning to the stories and characters of the New Testament for answers to life's questions, moral guidance, and encouragement to persevere in loyalty to God.

Mary and Joseph

Biblical Background

he Gospel accounts of Jesus' annunciation and birth (found in the books of Matthew and Luke) center on his importance as the Son of God. Mary is a vehicle for the Incarnation, but other than her song, the Magnificat (Luke 1:46–55), she has little to say in the narrative. Joseph is even more shadowy, providing a home and legal protection to Mary

Joseph and Mary

and the child Jesus, but little else. Naturally, this gave rise to speculation about the two, their lives prior to the birth of Jesus, and incidents that occurred shortly after Jesus' birth. Such an important couple deserved more attention than was to be found in the official accounts, so extra-biblical accounts were written to fill in the gaps.

The *Protevangelium of James*

A number of apocryphal works attempted to fill in some of the details about Mary and Joseph. One of the most popular was the *Protevangelium of James* (abbreviated *PJ*) that dates to the mid- to late second century A.D. The author claims to be James, the brother of Jesus, but a lack of knowledge about Jewish customs and a clear misunderstanding of Palestinian geography indicate that the author may have been a Syrian or Egyptian Christian. Most surviving manuscripts are written in Greek, although the popularity of the work is indicated by the many translations that exist and its citation in the works of such important early church fathers as Origen (died 254) and Clement of Alexandria (early third century). This work continued to be used as part of popular theology in the Eastern Orthodox Church for many centuries. However, it was condemned by the fourth-century historian and theologian Jerome for its mention of Joseph's previous marriage and children prior to his marriage to Mary. As a result, the Western church, based in Rome, attempted to suppress the material, but the *PJ* still had an impact on the growth of the theological importance of the Virgin Mary.

The Life of Mary

The story found in *PJ* is an attempt to provide the figure of Mary with a miraculous (although not immaculate) birth narrative. In this way, she receives her proper due as the mother of Jesus. The tale begins with a familiar theme, an old barren couple who miraculously receive a child from God. Joachim and Anna are righteous and God-fearing, but they have no children. To cleanse any possible sin from his spirit and to entreat God without any distractions, Joachim spends 40 days and 40 nights in the wilderness (compare this to Jesus' similar activity in Matthew 4:2). For her part, Anna dresses in mourning garments and laments the fact that she is unfulfilled. The prayers of this old couple are answered by an angel who predicts the birth of a child and promises that this infant "shall be spoken of in the whole world."

When Anna gives birth, she proclaims "my soul is magnified this day" (Mary's similar song can be

Answered Prayers

Elements in the story of Joachim and Anna are reminiscent of stories in the Old Testament and in other ancient Near Eastern literature. In the epic of Aqhat from the north Syrian port city of Ugarit (about 1600 B.C.), the righteous king Danil prays fervently to the gods and makes special sacrifices to them for seven days before they respond affirmatively to his plea for a son. In the story of Samson's parents, they learn of the birth of their son from an angel who appears to them separately (Judges 13:2–23), just as in the case of Anna and Joachim. Similarly, both Anna and Hannah, the mother of Samuel, promise to dedicate their hoped-for child to God's service if the Lord opens their wombs and allows them to conceive (1 Samuel 1:9–11).

found in Luke 1:46–55) and names the child Mary. The special nature of this child then is demonstrated by her being able to walk at six months. As a way of setting Mary apart from other children and protecting her purity, Joachim creates a kind of "sanctuary" within his house for her. He also employs the willing service of Hebrew virgins who

come to care for her. Their virginity is a model
of Mary's nature and signifies her eventual role as
Christ's mother. At her presentation in the temple
on her first birthday, the chief priests, scribes, and
elders bless her, while Anna, the aged mother,
rejoices in her ability to nurse Mary and sings a
song of thanksgiving (compare this to Elizabeth's
prayer in Luke 1:25).

As Mary grows older, her parents must make
the decision to present her to God as Anna had
promised. They delay this task until the child is
three years old and no longer is dependent on her
mother (a timing that is very similar to Samuel's
presentation after he is weaned in 1 Samuel 1:22–
28). Mary is taken to the temple in procession
with torch-bearing virgins and is greeted by the
high priest with a kiss and a blessing, which pre-
dicted that "because of you the Lord at the end of
the days will reveal his redemption to the sons of
Israel."

Mary remains as a ward in the temple, being fed
by the hand of an angel, until her 12th year. At that
point, as she nears puberty, the priests take council

because once her menstrual cycle begins she can no longer remain within the temple precincts (according to the law set forth in Leviticus 15:19–30). In order to determine God's will, Zacharias, the high priest, goes into the inner precinct in the temple, which is called the Holy of Holies, where an angel tells him to assemble all the widowers of the land. God will then indicate which of this company is chosen to become Mary's husband.

The priests gather the rod of each widower assembled there, and the high priest prays over them within the temple. The rods are then returned one by one. When Joseph the carpenter receives his rod, a dove emerges from it and comes to rest on his head, indicating that he is the chosen one of God. When presented with Mary as his ward by the high priest, Joseph is embarrassed and asks to be forgiven this responsibility. He says that he is an old man with sons by his first wife, and he does not wish to "become a laughingstock" among his neighbors. Zacharias warns him against attempting to cast aside God's command, and Joseph relents. However, as soon as he has taken

Mary home, Joseph leaves her so he can continue work on several building projects, saying "the Lord will guard you." The *Gospel of Pseudo-Matthew* adds here that Mary is accompanied to Joseph's house by six virgins so that she does not go unchaperoned and will not be left completely alone while Joseph is away.

The next step in creating an image of perfection for Mary by the author of the *Protevangelium of James* comes when the priests decide to commission the weaving of a veil for the temple. Only virgins of the lineage of David are allowed to participate, and at this point the reader is told that Mary is of that lineage. This may have been an answer to early criticism in the church that Matthew's genealogy for Joseph (Matthew 1:1–16) was insufficient proof of Jesus' kinship tie to David. If Mary is also given a Davidic lineage, however, these concerns are addressed and defused.

Given one of the favored tasks in the weaving process, Mary is interrupted in her work by an angel who tells her that she will miraculously conceive and bear the "Son of the Most High." Her initial willingness to serve as the "handmaid of the Lord" is similar to the canonical story (see Luke 1:38). However, this story next brings out a more human set of reactions—shock and fear. Mary goes to visit her cousin Elizabeth, who is pregnant with John the Baptist. Elizabeth addresses her as "the mother of my Lord," but somehow Mary has forgotten what the angel had told her. Mary is perplexed and afraid when she realizes that she is supposed to remain a virgin until marriage and yet has become pregnant at age 16.

Mary hides herself from view, but Joseph returns as she enters her sixth month and there is no way to prevent him from seeing her condition. Joseph berates himself for leaving her alone and thus available to temptation and defilement. When Mary assures him, tearfully, that she has not "known" a man, he is even more confused. After thinking it over, he plans to quietly "put her away," but this idea is immediately set aside when an angel appears and tells him the child is "of the Holy Spirit."

Despite Joseph's belief in Mary, the priests are not convinced. They accuse Mary of failing to uphold her honor, and they accuse Joseph of taking advantage of his ward, consummating their marriage without the benefit of a ceremony before the people. When Mary and Joseph continue to plead their innocence, the priests administer the "water of conviction" to each of them, leaving it up to

God to determine their guilt (see Numbers 5:12–22 for this method of trial by ordeal). Both pass the test without any sign of sin being displayed on their bodies, and the people rejoice at the power of God made manifest.

The angel bringing good news to Mary

The census of Caesar Augustus (Luke 2:1) forces Joseph and Mary to travel to Bethlehem, but before they reach the town Mary goes into labor. Joseph finds a cave where she may give birth and goes to seek a midwife. During his search, Joseph

experiences a miraculous stoppage of motion
around him. Sheep are frozen in place, a shepherd
stands with his staff raised, and birds are stopped in
midflight. Then, just as suddenly, all returns to nor-
mal and the midwife appears. Joseph tells her about
Mary and brings her to the cave. However, before
she can assist the birth, a cloud hides the cave and
then a bright light appears, blinding them tempo-
rarily. When the light dims, the child has been born
and the midwife cries out in astonishment.

The *Protevangelium of James* then repeats the story
of the three wise men following a star so bright
that it outshines all others. Herod's anger and concern lead to
the slaughter
of all babies
in the area
under two
years old.
While no
mention is
made here
of Mary and

The birth of John the Baptist

Joseph's flight to Egypt, the narrative does describe how Elizabeth is able to save the infant John the Baptist from Herod's forces by climbing into the hills. When she can go no farther, she prays. In response the "mountain is rent asunder" and a light held by an angel guides them to safety.

After Herod cannot find John, he has his officers question Zacharias, John's father. Zacharias denies any knowledge of where his son has gone, and Herod orders the father's execution. He is killed before the altar in the temple (there is a reference to this story in Matthew 23:35). Only his blood, however, now turned to stone, can be found there because his body had disappeared. A voice tells the frightened priests of Zacharias's murder, and three days of mourning follow. The narrative then concludes with the appointment of Symeon as the new high priest. A note is added that Symeon has received a message from the Holy Spirit that he would not die until he has seen Christ "in the flesh" (see Luke 2:25–26). In this way, the continuity of priestly leadership is tied to Christ's coming mission.

The *Gospel of Pseudo-Matthew*

The amount of additional information on Mary's early life continued to grow during the centuries of the medieval church. Among such works was the *Gospel of Pseudo-Matthew* (abbreviated *Ps-M*), which elaborates on previous sets of stories, such as those in *PJ,* augmenting the narrative in places.

Among the unique additions of the *Ps-M* is an encounter Joseph and Mary have on their way to Bethlehem. Mary says she has had a vision of two persons, one weeping and one rejoicing. Joseph

Magnifying Mary

The *Gospel of Pseudo-Matthew* is a Latin work that dates to the eighth or ninth century and is heavily dependant on the *Protevangelium of James* as well as other apocryphal infancy narratives. It does contain some unique material, but like the other works, its principal aim is to magnify the importance of Mary. Interestingly, the *Gospel of Pseudo-Matthew* contains fictional letters from two bishops to Jerome, the translator of the Vulgate, as a way of adding to its authenticity.

thinks she is merely jabbering and discounts what she says. But then a young man (an angel) appears. He scolds Joseph and tells them that the vision is of the "Jews weeping because they have departed from their God" and of the "gentiles rejoicing because they are now... near to the Lord."

This work also describes in some detail the flight to Egypt to escape Herod. The story presented in the *Ps-M* is filled with miraculous events, including several occasions when Jesus saves his parents from menacing beasts. In one episode, they are accosted by dragons, but the infant Jesus climbs down from his mother's lap and stands before the beasts. They fall down and worship him and then retire to their cave (this story provides an echo of Psalm 148:7, particularly in the King James Version). When his parents exclaim that Jesus must not place himself in such danger, he replies that he is not a mere child "for I have always been and even now am perfect." Later attacks by lions, leopards, and wolves end similarly, with the beasts worshipping Jesus.

Another miraculous event occurs when the group is forced to rest because Mary is overcome by the heat. Mary notices a palm tree laden with fruit, and she expresses a desire to eat some of it. Jesus causes the palm tree to bow down so that Mary can reach its fruit. When Joseph is concerned about their empty water bags, Jesus also has one of the tree's roots tap a nearby water source so the bags can be filled. For its helpfulness, the tree is rewarded by having a branch taken by an angel to be transplanted in Paradise. Stories such as these serve the purpose of demonstrating Jesus' respect for his parents while maintaining proof of his lordship over all creation.

When they reach Egypt, Mary and the child enter a temple. As they set foot inside, the 365 idols housed there are cast from their pedestals and broken (compare this to similar events in 1 Samuel 5:1–5). The local governor and all the people are so overcome by this sign of God's supremacy that they fall down and worship, acknowledging their belief "in the Lord God through Jesus Christ." Mary's role as the bearer of Christ is also highlighted since she is always described as holding Jesus to her breast as the people worship him.

The Death of Joseph

An abbreviated version of the narrative in *PJ* is found in the *History of Joseph the Carpenter*. The primary concern of this work, narrated by Jesus, is to describe the death of Joseph at the advanced age of 111 and again to have one of Jesus' parents acknowledge his true nature.

Jesus and Mary sit with Joseph on his deathbed, and Mary calls her daughter Lydia to join her in the mourning lament. When Death approaches to take Joseph away, Jesus rebukes him and holds him

The *History of Joseph the Carpenter*

The *History of Joseph the Carpenter* is another apocryphal narrative that deals with the parents of Jesus and is dependent on *PJ*. It was first written in Greek but survives as a Coptic text and thus is probably an Egyptian work. While its exact date of composition is unknown, some scholars suggest the fourth or fifth century. A later date, however, is suggested by its emphasis on the feast day of Joseph, something that was not established in the canonical calendar until a few centuries later.

at bay, behind the door, while they all pray that the journey Joseph's soul must take will be a safe one, that the "river of fire be as water and the sea of demons cease vexing." In his last moments, the old man makes his confession of faith in Jesus as the Son of God. He also asks forgiveness for doubting Mary's purity since he was ignorant of the circumstances of Jesus' conception. When Joseph dies, the angels Michael and Gabriel shroud his body in a shining cloth and preserve his soul from the demons of darkness until he can be conducted into the "dwelling place of the pious."

After Jesus tells them the story of Joseph's death, some of the apostles ask him why Joseph could not have been spared death like Enoch and Elijah. Jesus tells them that even these two witnesses of events on earth will eventually have to die, victims of the venom of the Antichrist. This mention of the "two witnesses" parallels the account in Revelation 11:1–7 and ties this work into the apocalyptic expectations of many Christians.

Stories of Jesus' Infancy

Biblical Background

uke's statement that "the child grew and became strong" (Luke 2:40) simply did not satisfy the need of early Christians to know more about their Savior's childhood. Certainly, the story of his presentation in the Temple and his conversation at age 12 with the elders (Luke 2:41–52) helped fill in a small gap between Jesus' birth and the beginning of his ministry, but it also served to whet believers' appetite for more. When the official accounts failed to give them what they felt they needed, the storytellers wove legends that eventually supplied most of the missing details. The growing popularity of these legendary stories during the Middle Ages can be interpreted in two ways: (1) as the occasional suppression of this material by the leaders of the church, and (2) as an explosion of religious art depicting such stories as Jesus' birth in a cave and Mary spinning a portion of the Temple veil.

Infancy Narratives

There are a number of Infancy Narratives that date to the second through sixth centuries A.D. The *Arabic Infancy Gospel* is of Egyptian origin, probably written originally in Syriac in the fifth century, and survives in a number of manuscripts as well as in the 13th-century "History of the Virgin." It is dependent for some of its material on the *Protevangelium of James* and the *Infancy Story of Thomas*. The *Life of John the Baptist* also contains some infancy material. The author claims that the document was written in Greek by the Egyptian bishop Serapion at the end of the fourth century, but it survives in Syriac manuscripts.

Jesus in Egypt

The flight to Egypt was undertaken to save Jesus from Herod's plan to kill all the infants in Bethlehem (Matthew 2:16–18). Although no mention is made in the Gospels of what transpired in Egypt, the apocryphal Infancy Stories contain numerous tales of the miracles the child Jesus performed. Most of these episodes are designed to show Jesus' mercy to the poor and afflicted.

Among the tales in the *Arabic Infancy Gospel* is one about Jesus' bathwater. After the child has been cleansed, a woman stores the water and later pours it on a girl who has leprosy. The girl is immediately cured, and the townspeople exclaim that Jesus and

The *Infancy Story of Thomas*

The most complete text describing Jesus' early childhood is found in the *Infancy Story of Thomas* (not to be confused with the Coptic Gospel of Thomas, which is not a narrative and simply contains sayings attributed to Jesus). The earliest versions of this document were written in Syriac and Greek, but a number of Latin manuscripts also exist. What is interesting to note is that each manuscript differs slightly from the others, suggesting both that there were multiple traditions and versions circulating and that the copyists felt free to add material they believed effectively expanded the stories. Its earliest date of composition is the second century A.D., but one may presume that stories were added to some manuscripts for at least two more centuries. The author, using Thomas's name to add authority to the document, was probably a gentile Christian.

his parents "are gods, not men." In a similar story, water from a spring is used to wash Jesus' shirt. As Mary wrings out the sweat from the laundered shirt, balsam appears in that place.

After leaving the village in which they had been staying, the holy couple is captured in the desert by a gang of robbers. One, named Titus, asks his fellow robber Dumachus to help him free Mary and Joseph and the child. Dumachus refuses until Titus pays him 40 drachma. After their escape, Jesus tells his mother that in 30 years these two robbers will be crucified on either side of him and that the kind Titus will be allowed to enter Paradise (see Luke 23:32–43).

Jesus the Miracle-Working Child

The *Infancy Story of Thomas* describes additional episodes about Jesus from ages five through twelve. Like the *Protevangelium of James,* this document chronicles a series of miracles by Jesus. However, *PJ* is always careful to tie each miracle, such as the submission of dragons and other beasts, to Jesus' mastery of creation, therefore making it a justification for his worship. Similarly, *Ps-M*'s infancy material attempts to show Jesus as master over Egypt's gods when their images are cast down and broken as Jesus and Mary enter a temple. *Thomas,* on the other hand, portrays a child Jesus who learns how to control his powers as he matures. Some of the stories, certainly, were told for entertainment and have less concern for ethical issues. In fact, some depict Jesus as an aloof and knowing child, who strikes out at ignorance and is very frightening to his parents, teachers, and playmates. However, the apparent theme here is to show Jesus experiencing some of the same phases of development that all children must pass through.

Perhaps because many Christians were experiencing persecution at the hands of kings and other powerful individuals, the authors of the Infancy Stories may have speculated about how Jesus handled his extraordinary powers as a child. This may explain why there is an obvious maturing process that takes place in the stories. Thus the five-year-old Jesus uses divine powers almost indiscriminately and without thought, while the more meditative twelve-year-old Jesus considers his actions much more carefully.

The opening tale has Jesus, like many little boys, playing beside a stream of water. He creates separate small pools of water, cleanses the water with a word, and then shapes seven sparrows from the clay and water of his pools. His almost absent-minded creative acts recall God's creation of Adam in Genesis 2:4–7. The story is not finished, however, because Jesus has performed these acts on the Sabbath, and as is so often the case in his later ministry, Jewish people nearby complain that he is violating the law (see similar situations in Matthew 12:1–12 and Mark 3:2–4). When Joseph comes to Jesus and asks him why he has done this "work" on the Sabbath, Jesus simply claps his hands and cries "Off with you!" and the clay sparrows come to life and fly away. The people are amazed by this sight and go to tell the Jewish elders.

While most are distracted by following the birds, the son of Annas the scribe takes a willow branch and destroys Jesus' pools. This makes Jesus very angry. He calls the boy a "godless dunderhead" and then curses him, causing him to be withered up like an old man. The stricken boy's parents carry him away and reproach Joseph for having a child capable of doing such things.

Another example of Jesus reacting angrily occurs when a boy runs past him and brushes Jesus' shoulder. In exasperation, Jesus stops the boy in his tracks with a word, and the child drops dead immediately. The grieving parents cannot believe that Jesus can make such a thing happen just by speaking angry words, and they warn Joseph that he will be driven from the village if he does not teach his son to control such power to curse. When Joseph attempts to instruct Jesus, the child absolves his father, saying that Joseph is not speaking his own words, but those of others. Then the people who had pressured Joseph are struck with blindness. Joseph cannot take any more, and he grabs Jesus by the ear hoping to get Jesus' attention and prevent any further damage, but Jesus simply tells Joseph not to "vex" him.

Such behavior on Jesus' part, lacking any apparent respect for his elders, brings Zacchaeus the teacher into the narrative. He tells Joseph that he will take the child and instruct him in his letters as well as in the proper way of addressing his elders. However, Jesus scorns Zacchaeus's ability to teach him anything. As they study the Greek alphabet, Jesus complains that his teacher does not know even the first thing about the true nature of Alpha (the first Greek letter), so how can he dare to go on to Beta (the second Greek letter)? Jesus then presents an allegorical explanation of Alpha's shape and properties that completely confounds Zacchaeus. He takes Jesus back to Joseph, saying, "I strove to get a disciple and have found myself with a teacher!" Jesus responds favorably to this humbling speech by Zacchaeus. He graciously heals all those children and their parents who had been afflicted by his word.

Two other teachers try to instruct Jesus, with very different results. The first tries pedantically to force Jesus to repeat his alphabet over and over. Jesus sees no value in this, and when he refuses to respond to his teacher's urging, the man strikes Jesus on the head. The boy curses him and leaves him in a coma. Joseph, fearing the reaction of the neighbors, takes Jesus home and hides him. The second teacher, however, is much more understanding of Jesus' abilities. When Jesus, with the help of the Holy Spirit, expounds authoritatively on the law, the teacher praises him, telling a frightened Joseph that the boy is full of grace and wis-

dom. And, because this man has spoken wisely, Jesus heals the foolish teacher.

The next episode again involves a testing of

Jesus in the temple

Jesus' powers and once again demands that the people acknowledge his word as supreme. While Jesus is playing with another child in the upper story of a house, his companion falls from a window and is killed. The parents accuse Jesus of pushing the child to his death. Jesus simply replies, "I did not throw him down." No one believes him, so Jesus leaps down beside the body of the dead boy, calls him by name, and instructs him to arise and tell everyone whether Jesus had pushed him. Miraculously, the boy gets up and affirms Jesus' innocence. Jesus is thus shown to display the same power to raise the dead that he will employ during his ministry (similar incidents occurred in Matthew 9:18–26 and Luke 7:11–17).

There is a final set of miracle stories contained in *Thomas,* each one showing Jesus' growing maturity and concern for others. Some, like the story of Jesus carrying water in his cloak when he falls and breaks his mother's water jar, display a small child's solution to a problem. In another case, Jesus shows his father that his powers can have a practical benefit. Joseph had received a commission to fashion a bed for a rich man. However, when the sections for a bed are cut, one beam is longer than the other. Jesus then steps in to help his father by miraculously stretching the shorter piece of wood so that both now match.

Domestic miracles are amusing to the audience and suggest Jesus' future potential to help all people. But it is in the stories where Jesus relieves suffering that his true maturity is demonstrated. For example, when a woodcutter wounds himself with his ax and is bleeding to death, Jesus runs forward and heals the injured foot. Similarly, when a viper bites Joseph's son James, Jesus breathes on the venom mark and James is cured while the snake bursts. Another time, Jesus hears the cries of mourning when a small child dies. He immediately runs to the house and revives the child, saying, "Do not die but live and be with your mother." He also raises a young man who had been killed in a construction accident. Such acts of charity show Jesus' mature harnessing of his power and emotions. No longer is Jesus shown to wield power on instinct. In these final stories he sets a tone very similar to that found in the Gospels.

Stories of Jesus' Ministry

Biblical Background

s is so often the case with public figures, the official narrative about their lives is an abridged one. The writers of the Gospels shaped the stories they told in such a way that Jesus' message and the signs of his power—the miracles—were highlighted. There was surely much more that could be said about the three years of Jesus' public ministry, but decisions were made to include only what we now see as the scriptures. What follows are the "other stories" about Jesus that somehow never made it into the Gospels but still survived to add color and additional dimensions to the founder of Christianity. In large part, they represent the Gospels used by several of the Jewish-Christian communities during the first three centuries of the Christian era. Cited in the works of the early church fathers such as Origen, Clement, Jerome, Eusebius, and Epiphanius, they are in most cases variants on the canonical Gospel of Matthew and include some heretical beliefs that would eventually be condemned by the church councils. Some of these variations on the Gospel story are the result of Christian communities borrowing elements of other religions and their sacred stories and blending them with the narratives about Jesus. In some cases, this was done to make conversion to Christianity easier, and in other cases it may be the result of an attempt to further enhance Jesus' position as the Son of God.

The *Gospel of the Nazareans*
Aside from a few fragments, all that is known of the *Gospel of the Nazareans* (*GN*) comes from citations in various church fathers' works and in their commentaries on books of the New Testament. For example, Jerome, the translator of the Latin Vulgate edition and premier scholar of the latter half of the fourth century A.D., cites a passage from the *GN* indicating that Jesus, despite the urging of his mother, did not intend to be baptized by John the Baptist, saying, "Wherein have I sinned that I should go and be baptized by him?" This stands in

stark contrast to Matthew 3:13–15, in which Jesus has to convince John to baptize him.

Similarly, in his commentary on the story of the man with the withered hand (Matthew 12:9–13), Jerome cites the *GN* where it adds the information that the man was a mason. His plea to Jesus to heal him is based on his desire to return to his profession and earn a living rather than continue to exist as a beggar. An eighth- or ninth-century source notes that the *GN* names this mason Malchus. While these are relatively minor additions, they do serve to flesh out the story of an anonymous sufferer. Giving the man a profession and a name makes it easier for the listener or the reader to identify with his pain and perhaps to associate it with their own.

Occasionally these citations appear to be trying to answer a question that has either been asked by one of the church fathers' students or was a long-standing query. An example of this may be a note in a 14th-century text describing Jesus' passion narrative. In John 18:15–16, while Jesus is being questioned by Caiaphas, the high priest, Peter and "another disciple known to the high priest" stood outside. The *GN* supplies the information that the unnamed disciple is John and that he is known to the high priest because his father Zebedee had often sent him to the high priest's palace with fish for their table. It also notes here that Peter was not only standing outside the door, but he was weeping loudly before he was allowed to come into the palace.

An anti-Jewish bias is illustrated in some of these fragments. In one case the story of Jesus' scourging by the Roman soldiers (Mark 15:15) is expanded to include the accusation that Jews had bribed the four soldiers to beat Jesus even more severely than usual. Thus his blood flows "from every part of his body." These same four men are also bribed to inflict greater cruelty as they crucify Jesus (four soldiers are also portrayed in John 19:17–24).

Some final variations noted in the *GN* include the statement that, after Jesus absolves his executioners ("Father, forgive them; for they know not what they do"—Luke 23:34), thousands of those standing around the cross are converted to

Christianity. One church father, Haimo of Auxerre, says it is thousands of Jews who are converted, while a 14th-century medieval source points to the 3,000 people converted on the day of Pentecost (Acts 2:41) and an additional 5,000 at a later date (Acts 4:4). In addition, the signs of mourning at the moment of Jesus' death, expressed by unnatural darkness and the tearing of the temple veil in Luke 23:44–45, are replaced in the *GN* by the splitting of the huge lintel stone of the temple and the wailing of disembodied voices. This latter variation on the traditional story is also found in *Jewish Antiquities* by the first-century historian Josephus. Since the lintel would have been in full view of the public (the veil was seen only by the priests within the temple), it would have been a much more effective piece of evidence of Jesus' importance and power.

The *Gospel of the Ebionites*

The *Gospel of the Ebionites* (*GE*) represents a variant gospel that reflects the views of the Jewish-Christian Ebionite community. They retain some aspects of their Jewish heritage—evidence of this can be seen in the story of Jesus' choosing his 12 disciples. This recounting resembles that of Luke 6:13–16, although it is written with Jesus as the narrator. As is the case in the canonical Gospels, the number 12 is emphasized, demonstrating a parallel with the 12 tribes of Israel and the Jewish origin of each document.

However, many of the Ebionite ideas would later be considered heretical. For instance, since the Ebionites denied the doctrine of the virgin birth, Jesus is portrayed as no more than a man until he is invested with divine power when the Holy Spirit unites with him at the time of his baptism by John the Baptist (based on Matthew 3:14–17). The "Christ" is therefore

The baptism of Jesus

created by this union. It is at this point, rather than through the incarnation with Mary, that Jesus becomes a divine being. In this episode the voice from heaven proclaims Jesus to be "my Beloved Son" when Jesus emerges from the water and again when John questions Jesus to ascertain who he is. Further clarifying this position, the Ebionites are also said to deny that Christ was "begotten of God the Father" but was "created as one of the arch-angels" to rule over all the other angels and all the creatures of God. In this way, the nativity stories are completely set aside, and Jesus' role as the bearer of a new revelation directly from God is reinforced.

John the Baptist is also portrayed in a slightly different way, with his traditional diet reduced from locusts and wild honey (Matthew 3:4) to simply honey. This emphasizes the vegetarian doctrine of the Ebionite community. A further sign of this adherence to a vegetarian diet is found in Jesus' refusal to eat the meat of the Passover meal at the Last Supper (compare this to Luke 22:15). By having him refuse to eat meat, and by having Jesus say that he has "come to do away with sacrifices," they emphasize Jesus' role as the ultimate sacrifice. It also provides justification for their adherence to a special vow to eat no meat or perhaps to prevent any possible violation of the Jewish dietary laws.

The *Gospel of the Hebrews*

The emphasis placed on the person of James, the brother of Jesus, in the *Gospel of the Hebrews* (GH) suggests that this document served the spiritual needs of the Jewish-Christian community in Egypt just as the Gospel of Luke served the gentile communities of the early church. James, the leader of the Jewish-Christian church in Jerusalem (Acts 15:13; Galatians 1:19), would have been a particularly important figure to those Jewish-Christian groups who wished to continue strict adherence to Jewish practice in addition to Christian doctrine.

Here again there is a difference in the perception of Jesus' fully divine nature. In one Coptic fragment from a letter by Cyril of Jerusalem, Christ is described as a preexistent being who made the decision to "come upon the earth to men" and is aided in doing this by the angel Michael, at God the Father's direction. Mary is also described as a "power come into the world," and thus she also has a preexistent divine nature. The effort here seems to be to divorce Jesus from his human nature, which also requires Mary, as his mother, to set aside her humanity.

Jesus' baptism, as in the *GE,* provides the moment in which the Christ is united with the Holy Spirit. It seems here that the Spirit had attempted to reside or "rest" in "all the prophets" but had only found true "rest" in Jesus. Quoting Psalm 132:14—"This is my rest forever: here will I dwell"—the *GH* is able to tie Jesus both to the theme of the hope of the people to return to Zion (Jerusalem as well as God's presence) and to the Christian idea of Messiah (the Spirit's ability to join with or merge in full with Jesus, thereby allowing his full powers to be made known).

A fragment of the Temptation narrative comparable to that in Matthew 4:8 is also contained here. In Matthew, the devil transports Jesus to the mount of temptation. However, in the *GH,* Jesus describes, perhaps to his disciples, how his "mother, the Holy Spirit" took him by the hair (compare this to Ezekiel's experience in Ezekiel 8:3) and transported him to Mount Tabor. Naming the Holy Spirit as his mother both follows the Hebrew or Aramaic notion of the spirit or "lady wisdom" as female and agrees with the idea of the Spirit's merging with Jesus at the time of his baptism.

The *Acts of John*

One final extrabiblical source for the ministry of Jesus is found in the *Acts of John (AJ)*, a document that was banned by the Church Council of A.D. 787. Because of this, only a portion of it survives in Greek and Latin texts and in scholarly citations and commentaries. It was probably written between A.D. 180 and 230 in the area of northern Syria. The work as a whole deals with the ministry of John, the son of Zebedee, in Asia Minor, but the portion described below contains his testimony about Jesus.

The narrative begins with Jesus calling the disciples to his service. What makes this version unusual is Jesus' shifting appearance. The *Acts of John* provides this dialogue between James and John that demonstrates some of the prospective disciples' confusion. James asks his brother, "What does he want, this child on the shore who called us?" John is mystified because the person he sees beckoning them is a young, handsome man with a cheerful face. They bring the boat to shore thinking their

Jesus calling his disciples

long night of fishing has affected their eyes. But as they come ashore they continue to see different things. James sees a young man whose beard has just begun to grow, while John sees an old, bald-headed man with a long flowing beard.

Even after they join his group of disciples, the changeable nature of Jesus' appearance continues to perplex John. He never sees Jesus shut his eyes, and at times it appears that Jesus is continually looking up toward heaven. When they recline for a meal, Jesus would regularly draw John close (as he also does in John 13:23). However, at times it would appear that Jesus' body was "smooth and soft" to the touch and at other times it felt like stone. These examples demonstrate that the author of the *Acts of John* understood Jesus' nature as quite mysterious and more like that of God than of man.

Another episode is a variation on the story of the transfiguration found in each of the synoptic Gospels (Matthew 17:1–8; Mark 9:2–8; Luke 9:28–36). As in those accounts, the disciples accompanying Jesus are dazzled by a blinding light. However, in the *AJ,* John exercises the same curiosity that any person might have. He creeps up behind Jesus and is able to see him standing in the light, stripped of his human garments and with a very inhuman guise. His feet are so white that the ground is lit by them. John is frightened by this transformation of his master, and he cries out. His inquisitiveness will earn him no rewards. Jesus grabs hold of his beard and rebukes him, and John suffers for 30 days from the pain of that "playful tug" on his beard.

On other occasions, John is further amazed by the abilities and nature of Jesus. Miracles seem to come very easily to him. For instance, he feeds his disciples from a single loaf when they dine, a clear parallel to the "feeding of the 4,000" in Mark 8:1–9. More mysterious, however, was the nature of Jesus' physical body. Sometimes when John touched Jesus, his body was like that of other men. But there were also times when that same touch encountered nothing material, as if Jesus did not exist in the flesh. John also notes that Jesus never seemed to leave behind any footprints, no matter how soft the ground was where he stepped.

Each of these tales magnifies the person of Jesus, in most instances beyond any mere human nature. It was difficult for those in the early church to deal with the idea of Jesus being both human and divine. The stories in these Jewish-Christian gospels and in the *Acts of John* suggest that many Christians felt more comfortable with a totally divine Jesus than with a God made human.

Jesus' Trial, Death, and Resurrection

Biblical Background

he central mystery of Christianity is the death and resurrection of Jesus, believed to be the consummation of his ministry of reconciling humanity to God. There remained something of a scandal, however, in the idea of a Messiah who was put on trial by his own people and condemned to a degrading death. Retellings of that experience found new ways to affirm Jesus' dignity and innocence. Moreover, the Gospels are silent about the time between Jesus' death and resurrection. This silence gave rise to imaginative legends about activities both in the land of the living and in the abode of the dead. The Acts of the Apostles speaks of Jesus remaining with the disciples for 40 days after his resurrection, but the biblical accounts of that period are rather sparse. Expansions and additions arose in an attempt to provide more windows into that formative time for the disciples—Jesus' final preparations for their work of building the kingdom of God on earth.

The Trial of Jesus

The expanded version of Jesus' trial before Pilate incorporates charges and suspicions raised about Jesus during his ministry that go strangely unmentioned in the record of the trial reported in the canonical Gospels. Throughout his ministry, Jesus was faced with questions about his birth (raised by Jewish leaders in John's Gospel, 8:39–41), and accusations concerning the breaking of Sabbath laws and being in league with the devil (see Matthew 12:9–14, 22–32; Luke 13:10–17). In the canonical Gospels, the trial charges focus on Jesus as a revolutionary, a pretender to royal power, and thus a threat to Rome; the *Acts of Pilate* gathers all the accusations made against Jesus by his fellow Jews throughout the Gospels. Jesus' innocence of all these charges is emphasized in this apocryphal text. The *Acts* also gives voice to the many people who were healed by Jesus. The reader of the canonical

Gospels asks, "Where did all Jesus' supporters and beneficiaries go?" Now they are brought into the events of Jesus' last days as witnesses for the defense, heightening the drama of the trial. The *Acts of Pilate* helps to make the trial of Jesus a more natu-

ral outgrowth of the canonical records of his ministry, as well as to affirm Jesus' innocence, kingly status, and divinity.

Pilate presiding over the trial of Jesus

As the *Acts of Pilate* opens, the chief priests and other members of the ruling council gather before Pilate. They accuse Jesus (whom they all know to have been born to Mary and Joseph, a mere carpenter) of claiming to be a king and the Son of God, profaning the Sabbath day, and seeking to overturn the Jewish law. When Pilate inquires about the precise nature of Jesus' breaking of the Sabbath laws, the priests reply that he has healed all manner of diseases when it was forbidden to heal on the Sabbath. They also claim that he healed diseases and cast out demons by means of sorcery.

Pilate sends for Jesus to be brought in "with gentleness," presuming his innocence of wrongdoing. When Pilate's messenger sees Jesus, he recognizes Jesus as the one whom the Jewish people greeted as king just days before. He therefore bows to Jesus and spreads out his cloak on the ground for Jesus to walk upon, as he had seen the crowds revere him. The priests are enraged at this display, but the messenger defends himself by explaining to Pilate how the Jewish people themselves had honored Jesus.

A second—and more impressive—token of respect comes from the most unexpected of places. Several soldiers are present in Pilate's courtroom serving as standard-bearers. These standards were the symbols of Roman rule and generally were long poles displaying a metal cameo of the emperor's image and other symbols of Rome such as

an eagle, all decorated with red drapes. As soon as
Jesus walks into Pilate's judgment hall, the standards
bow down to Jesus in reverence. Pilate is amazed
and calls the priests' attention to this sign, but they
respond that the soldiers must have lowered the
poles themselves. The soldiers deny it, claiming to
be pious worshippers of the Greek and Roman
gods. Pilate orders the Jews to select six strong men
to hold the standards upright and then has Jesus
brought in again. Once more, despite the efforts of
the Jews who struggle to keep the poles upright,
the standards bow down to do homage before
Jesus.

This supernatural sign fills Pilate with fear, and
at this moment word comes to him from his wife
not to have anything to do with Jesus, for he is
an innocent man (this message is also depicted in
Matthew 27:19). The priests claim that this is a sure
sign Jesus is a sorcerer. They resume their list of
charges, claiming that Jesus was born out of wedlock, that he was the cause of the deaths of many
children in Bethlehem, and that Joseph and Mary
fled to Egypt to get away from the disgrace of

Judas and His Wife

The *Acts of Pilate,* written during the fifth century A.D., contains substantially older traditions than some of the other writings. This text has been passed down as the first half of the *Gospel of Nicodemus.*

One aspect of Jesus' passion not touched on by the *Acts of Pilate* is Judas's betrayal of his teacher. A fragment from a Coptic passion narrative implicates Judas's wife in the plan to betray Jesus. Judas was accustomed to stealing from the common purse of Jesus' disciples, taking the ill-gotten gain home to share with his wife. One day, hoping for greater financial reward, she urged Judas to betray his master to the authorities. Judas "listened to her as Adam did to Eve" and made plans with the chief priests. This tradition resonates with attempts throughout the history of the synagogue and the church to explain the evils of men by pointing to the greater evils of women.

being fornicators. Twelve Jews step forward, however, saying that they were present for the betrothal of Mary and Joseph, proving that Jesus was not born out of wedlock. Pilate takes these 12 men aside and asks why the priests are so vehement in their charges. They respond that the priests act out of jealousy, because Jesus healed on the Sabbath day. Jesus is on trial, in effect, because of his noble works.

The trial now continues much as it does in the canonical Gospels, with charges concerning the temple and blasphemy being introduced. At this, a number of witnesses for the defense arise. Nicodemus, known from the Gospel of John as a sympathizer if not a disciple of Jesus (John 3:1–15; 19:39–40), steps forward and tells Pilate that he tried to dissuade the priests from bringing Jesus to trial, saying that if Jesus' works were not from God they would amount to nothing. The priests reproach Nicodemus angrily. Another witness stands up, telling how Jesus healed him of paralysis. The priests point out that this healing happened on a Sabbath. A second witness tells how Jesus healed him from blindness as he sat beside the road to Jerusalem, and he is followed by a man who was healed from lameness and another who was cured of leprosy. Finally, the voice of the woman who was healed of a flow of blood that persisted for 12 years

is heard from the distance, but the priests can only
reply that they do not accept women's testimony
in court. The verdict, however, must be the same.
The story returns to the well-known plot of the
canonical Gospels, recounting how Pilate declares
Jesus' innocence but hands him over to execution
all the same so as to avoid a riot.

Joseph of Arimathea and the Mystery of the Resurrection

The canonical Gospels give little indication of
how the chief adversaries of Jesus reacted to the
pious acts of Joseph of Arimathea and Nicodemus
or, more specifically, to the rumors of Jesus being
raised from the dead. The second half of the *Acts
of Pilate* fills in this gap for its readers. It invents a
tale of mystery as the chief priests and Sanhedrin
attempt to piece together what really happened
to Jesus' body and, when they face the inevitable
conclusion, how they are still able to reject Jesus'
messiahship.

Joseph of Arimathea is known from all four
canonical Gospels as the man who gave Jesus a

proper burial, saving his corpse from the disgrace of being left unburied. He was, John tells us, a "disciple of Jesus, but secretly for fear" of the Jewish leaders (John 19:38). In the *Acts of Pilate* Joseph's fears are substantiated. The chief priests send armed guards to arrest him for tending Jesus' body, and they also plan to arrest Nicodemus and the 12 men who bore witness to Jesus' good works in Pilate's courtroom. Joseph is taken late on Friday, presumably on his return from the gravesite, and kept in a "windowless room" under guard during the Sabbath. The Jewish leaders plan to meet on the first day of the week (Sunday) to determine the manner of his execution. When they return after the Sabbath, they find the guards at their posts and the seal on the door intact. They do not, however, find Joseph, who has mysteriously disappeared from a windowless room. After this, they abandon their plans to arrest the other men who had spoken on Jesus' behalf.

As they are pondering what happened to Joseph, the guards posted at Jesus' tomb arrive, telling the familiar story from Matthew's Gospel—the

appearance of an angel who rolled away the stone
at the mouth of the tomb, the visit of the women
who followed Jesus, and the announcement that
Jesus had risen. The chief priests chide the guards
for not arresting the women and offer them a
large sum of money to keep quiet and spread the
rumor that the disciples stole the body (which is
also reported in Matthew 28:12–14). After this,
however, three pious Jews (a priest, a Levite, and a
rabbi) come to the Jewish leaders, saying that they
saw Jesus speaking with his disciples, commissioning them to spread the gospel, and being taken up
to heaven. Once again, the chief priests give out
large sums of money in an attempt to seal their lips.

Nicodemus reminds the council of the ascen-
sion of Elijah into heaven and how the people
diligently searched for Elijah in the mountains for
three days (2 Kings 2:15–18). He suggests that they
do the same for Jesus, to test the truth of the report
that he was taken up into heaven. After comb-
ing the countryside, the priests' servants fail to
find Jesus. They have, however, found Joseph in his
hometown of Arimathea. Joseph is brought back to

the chief priests, who ask pardon for their attempts to kill him. The priests ask to learn what happened to him that night in the prison. Joseph tells them

that at midnight there was a flash of lightning and a shaking of the house in which he was being guarded. Someone took him by the hand and,

The risen Christ speaking with his disciples

supposing it to be a phantom, Joseph started reciting the commandments—an act that should make phantoms flee. When this figure began saying the commandments as well, Joseph looked up and saw that it was Jesus. Jesus took Joseph from the cell to the empty tomb and, finally, to Joseph's home.

At this report, the synagogue rulers and chief priests are greatly disturbed. One of them, named Levi, remembers that Jesus' parents were pious

and Torah-observant people. When Jesus was
born, they brought him to the Temple to Simeon,
Levi's teacher, who called the child "a light to
bring revelation to the Gentiles, and the glory of
Your people Israel" (Luke 2:32, NKJV; for the
full context, see Luke 2:28–35). Levi also recalls
that Simeon prophesied that the child would be
rejected. This prompts the chief priests to send
once again for the three witnesses to Jesus' ascen-
sion. Examining them separately, the priests find
that their testimony agrees in every respect and so
must be accepted as the truth. Annas and Caiaphas,
however, speak against the possibility that this Jesus
was God's anointed one. Laying aside the testimony
of Joseph and the others, they point to his shameful
execution on the cross. The priests together affirm
the judgment pronounced in Deuteronomy 21:23:
"he that is hanged [upon a tree] is accursed of
God," making reference to the cross. They therefore go out from their meeting room and warn all
Israel not to worship "created beings alongside the
Creator," thus applying the prohibition of idolatry
to the adoration of Jesus.

The Harrowing of Hell

Matthew records that, when Jesus died, not only was the sun darkened and the earth shaken, but also "the graves were opened; and many bodies of the saints which slept arose, and came out of the graves after his resurrection, and went into the holy city (Jerusalem), and appeared unto many" (Matthew 27:52–53). Here was a tantalizing and mysterious scene. Who were these people? Why would they be restored to life? Why would they not appear until after Jesus' resurrection? The Christians who shaped the stories that were later preserved in the *Gospel of Nicodemus* found here an answer to a very troubling theological question. If salvation is available only though Jesus, what happened to those who died before Jesus' ministry and crucifixion? Were the famous figures from the Old Testament accepted into heaven apart from Christ? If not, were they doomed forever to be excluded from heaven? To address these concerns, stories developed about Jesus' ministry not only to the living, but also concerning his proclamation to the dead between his crucifixion and his resurrection.

Jesus and the Righteous Dead

The idea that Jesus was still actively working out the redemption of people during the three days between his crucifixion and resurrection may go all the way back to the first century. The First Letter of Peter may allude to this when it speaks of "the gospel preached to them that are dead" (1 Peter 4:6). The apocryphal *Gospel of Peter* and *Letter of the Apostles,* both dated by the majority of scholars to the second half of the second century A.D., also speak of Jesus' visit to the righteous dead and their liberation from "the rest which is below" (limbo) to the repose of heaven. The *Gospel of Peter* presents this powerfully. As Jesus arises and exits his tomb, the cross itself follows. A voice from heaven asks, "Did you preach to those who sleep?" The cross answers: "Yes." The most detailed and, in many respects, most beautiful account of this story is preserved as part two of the *Gospel of Nicodemus,* which contains two originally independent works—the *Acts of Pilate* and the *Descent into Hell.* Given their present shape during the fifth century, these texts preserve substantially older traditions. Parts of them, at least, were known to Epiphanius in the late fourth century and may have been known as early as Justin in the mid-second century.

Simeon, previously mentioned as the high priest, and his two sons are among those who return from the dead after Jesus' resurrection. The story is told by his two sons, Karinus and Leucius, who wrote down a record of all they saw while they were in the underworld. The story goes as follows: At midnight on Good Friday, Abraham points out to the other patriarchs the approach of a bright light into the dark realm of the dead. Isaiah sees it and says that this is the light coming from God of which he prophesied during his life, saying, "The people that walked in darkness have seen a great light" (Isaiah 9:2). John the Baptist joins the growing circle of those looking toward this light and says, "This is the Lamb of God, to whom I bore witness in life, and God sent me here to prepare you as well to receive the only-begotten Son of God." John urges all to worship Jesus upon his arrival and to make use of the unique opportunity they are being given to repent of their worship of idols in life and to receive deliverance through Jesus.

At this point Adam urges his son Seth to tell all who are in Hades (the Greek underworld, or

"hell") about the prophecy Seth had received.
When Adam was dying, he sent Seth to the angel
who guarded the entrance to Eden to ask for some
of the oil from the tree of mercy, so that he might
anoint Adam and heal him. The angel told Seth
that it was not possible for Adam to be healed now,
but that in 5,500 years the Son of God would take
on human form and anoint Adam himself, cleans-
ing his descendants, healing their diseases, and
pouring out the Holy Spirit upon them.

While all the dead prepare themselves to receive
Jesus, Satan gravely tells Hades (hell is here presented as a living creature with a mouth and a belly,
in which the souls are trapped) about a certain Jew
who is on his way. This man caused Satan great
trouble while he was living, casting out Satan's
minions, healing disease, and even raising the dead.
Hades is afraid that their combined power will not
be sufficient to hold such a man, but Satan remains
sure of himself. Hades remembers that, just a short
time before, a man named Lazarus had been pulled
out of his belly, flying out like an eagle. Hades takes
Lazarus to be a bad sign of what this Jesus might

do if they allow him to enter the abode of the dead. He suggests that the best plan would be to keep Jesus out.

While Satan and Hades are speaking, a loud voice shouts, quoting Psalm 24:7, "Lift up your

heads, O ye gates; and be ye lift up, ye everlasting doors; and the King of glory shall come in!" Hades urges Satan and all his demons to bar the doors

Jesus raising Lazarus from the grave

to hell and prevent Jesus from coming in, but at the name of Jesus the gates of hell fly off their hinges. The angels bind Satan in chains, and Jesus orders Hades to imprison Satan until the second coming. Hades sharply rebukes Satan for orchestrating Jesus' crucifixion and death, since by dying he is now able to come down to pillage the underworld of all its souls: "All those whom you have gained for yourself by the tree of knowledge, in which Adam and Eve sinned, you have now lost through the tree of the cross."

The King of Glory then takes Adam by the hand and calls out to the rest: "All you who died through the tree which this man touched, come with me to paradise through the tree of the cross." The patriarchs, prophets, martyrs, and all the righteous who had come before follow with joy and, upon entering heaven, find Enoch and Elijah already there, together with the thief who died with Jesus and received the promise of paradise (Luke 23:43). The two brothers, Karinus and Leucius, are sent with the rest of the dead to be baptized in the Jordan, are allowed enough time to complete their witness to Jesus' liberation of the dead, and then vanish from sight.

The story, though obviously nonhistorical, nevertheless gives expression to some basic Christian teaching. Jesus' crucifixion marked the end of Satan's power and the grave's threat. Even those ultimate enemies, death and hell, were henceforward powerless against God's own. The story also allowed believers to affirm both that there was no salvation apart from Jesus and that the righteous people who died before Christ were not excluded from God's mercy and deliverance.

Jesus After the Resurrection

The Gospels and Acts record that Jesus spent 40 days with his disciples after his resurrection. During this time, he convinces them of the reality of his return (Mark 16:9–14; John 20:11–29; Acts 1:3); teaches them to read the Old Testament as a prophecy of his suffering, death, and resurrection (Luke 24:25–27, 44–47); and gives them instructions concerning their future work (Matthew 28:18–20; Mark 16:15–18; Acts 1:8). A number of early Christians expanded the traditions about what must have been an extremely momentous period of time. Surely Jesus had more to say to his disciples before returning to heaven, leaving to them the work of establishing the church!

The *Apocryphon of James* lengthens the time that Jesus spent with his disciples after his resurrection from 40 to 550 days, during which time they discussed the interpretation of Jesus' sayings and received additional teaching. At one point, the disciples ask to be spared the assaults of Satan. Jesus answers that there is no merit for them if they obey him without enduring Satan's attacks. If they obey in the midst of sufferings, however, God will love them as he does Jesus and will make them equal to him who first bore suffering, death, and shame unjustly. "Cease being lovers of the flesh, and afraid of sufferings," counsels Jesus. Words like this were meant to encourage believers in increasingly trying times—the endurance of suffering for the sake of Jesus was not an evil to be avoided, but an opportunity to demonstrate loyalty and to endear oneself with God through obedience and constancy.

The connection between Jesus and Paul—or, more specifically, the lack of such a connection— was a problem for Paul during his own apostolic ministry and remained a matter of concern for the church thereafter. Paul was conscious of the abnormal manner of his commissioning by Jesus as an apostle. He was not a witness of Jesus' ministry and resurrection but asserted that he had indeed met the risen Jesus in a vision and thus received his commission and qualifications (1 Corinthians 15:5–8; Galatians 1:11–16). The *Letter of the Apostles* tries to forge a closer and more direct link between Jesus and Paul. Between his resurrection and return to heaven, Jesus prophesies to his disciples that he will raise up a Jew named Paul, who will persecute the church but will be dramatically converted and, in turn, preach the gospel to the gentiles and be handed over to martyrdom. The disciples are instructed to teach Paul what they know about the fulfillment of the scriptures in Jesus to equip him for his apostleship. The detail that Paul learns about Jesus from the other disciples also serves to underscore the unity and agreement of the apostles. Texts such as 1 Corinthians and the Letter to the Galatians could easily give the impression that Paul was at odds with the chief apostles (Peter, James, and John), but it was increasingly important for the church to assert the harmony of the apostolic witness.

The Trial of Pilate

The man who sentenced Jesus to death has had a rather ambiguous and shadowy reputation in Christian circles. On the one hand, a number of Gospels portray him as going out of his way to try to release Jesus (Matthew and John, especially). He is forced by the Jewish leaders, however, to judge against his own conscience. On the other hand, since he had rendered an unjust verdict, it did not seem fair that he should go on to retire comfortably to a villa in Sicily. It is true that God's will was accomplished through Pilate, and Jesus almost acquits Pilate of all responsibility for the verdict he gave (John 19:11). However, Pilate condemns the Messiah to a brutal and shameful form of execution. The ambiguous attitude toward Pilate is perhaps most poignantly expressed in the *Paradosis Pilati* ("Tradition of Pilate"), known from 12th-century manuscripts but thought to preserve a much more ancient tradition.

Pilate sends a report to Roman Emperor Tiberius concerning the miracles that Jesus performed, the omens that accompanied Jesus' death,

Additional Legends About Pilate

What became of Pilate greatly occupied the imaginations of early Christians. The author of the *Letter of Pilate to Claudius* (possibly written as early as the end of the second century) recruits Pilate as a witness to Jesus' innocence, the malicious motives of the chief priests, and the resurrection itself. Christians in the Coptic (Egyptian) church regarded Pilate as a saint, "blessed" by God for having all God's promises fulfilled in his jurisdiction. Later medieval legends expand on the story of Pilate's trial, adding details about the illness of the emperor, who is healed by the handkerchief that Veronica used to wipe the sweat and blood from the face of Jesus as he was marched to Golgotha. These legends are marked by greatly increased venom toward Pilate as well as toward the Jewish people—so much so that the destruction of Jerusalem in A.D. 70 is attributed not to Roman suppression of a Jewish revolt but as punishment for the execution of Jesus.

and Pilate's discomfort about the verdict he was forced to render in order to forestall a revolt. The darkness and earthquake experienced at the hour of Jesus' death in Judea (Matthew 27:45, 51) also affected Rome and the entire Mediterranean. When Tiberius learns that Pilate was the cause of these ill omens, he orders him arrested and brought to stand trial before the senate in Rome. Tiberius rebukes Pilate for following the advice of the Jewish priests and mob, censuring him for not protecting a man who had done such marvelous acts as Jesus had and sending him to Rome. At the mention of the name of Jesus, the idols in the senate chamber fall down and crumble, which causes great fear to fall upon all assembled there.

On the following day, Pilate is once more brought before the senate and asked why he committed this injustice against Jesus. He replies that he did it because of the "seditious and lawless nature" of the Jewish people, for he feared that they would attempt an armed uprising if he did not give them their way. At this, Tiberius orders Licinius, the "chief governor of the East," to destroy the Jewish nation and scatter the Jews as slaves among the nations (which is a gross anachronism, as the Roman devastation of Jerusalem took place

30 years after Tiberius died and for very different reasons).

Pilate himself is sentenced to die, together with his wife Claudia Procula. As he stands at the place of his execution, he prays silently to Jesus to be forgiven for his action against him, pleading once more that he was forced into it by the "wicked Hebrews" who were planning to revolt. A voice greets him from heaven, saying that all generations of gentiles shall call him favored since, during his administration, all the words of the prophets were fulfilled. Pilate will be called to stand as Jesus' witness on the Day of Judgment, when Jesus comes to judge the 12 tribes of Israel. Pilate is then beheaded. His wife sees an angel descend from heaven to take up his head in a shroud and, filled with joy, she dies and is buried with her husband.

Peter, the Apostle of Jesus

Biblical Background

n the canonical Gospels and Acts, Simon Peter stands out from the rest of Jesus' followers. Formerly a fisherman, he became one of Jesus' first four disciples. Frequently in the Gospels he opens his mouth only to show his lack of insight into Jesus' ministry, but he is also the first disciple to speak the confession that Jesus is the "Christ, the Son of the living God" (Matthew 16:16). He is part of the inner circle of disciples— only he, James, and John witness the transfiguration of Jesus (Mark 9:2–8), and they are closest to Jesus as he prays in the Garden of Gethsemane before his arrest (Mark 14:32–42). Jesus names Peter the "rock" on which Jesus' church will be founded (a play on words—the Greek word for "rock" is *petra*).

Peter often failed to live up to the confidence that Jesus placed in him. Though he is the first to

confess Jesus as the Messiah, he is also the first to
reveal that he does not understand Jesus' messi-
anic ministry (Matthew 16:21–23). He makes the
loudest promises of remaining loyal unto death
at the Last Supper, but before the next morning
he denies three times that he even knows Jesus
(Matthew 26:31–35, 69–75). Nevertheless, after
his encounter with the resurrected Jesus, Peter
emerges as the leader of the disciples and, as the
circle grows, of the Jerusalem church during its
first years. Following his departure from Jerusalem
in A.D. 44, however, the New Testament reveals
very little. Aside from a few isolated incidents, such
as his confrontation with Paul at Antioch (Galatians
2:11–14), Peter largely drops out of the picture.

His prominence in the Gospels, his courageous
and charismatic deeds in Acts, and reports about his
bravery in Rome before his martyrdom led many
Christians to regard Peter as a hero. Since he was a
"pillar" among the apostles (Galatians 2:9), legends
about his exploits and extrabiblical reports of his
teachings circulated and gained a surprising degree
of authority during the second and third centuries.

Peter's Vision of Hell

An important and influential writing ascribed to Peter was the *Apocalypse of Peter.* Christian apocalypses (after the canonical Revelation) tended to serve the purpose of moral instruction. The *Apocalypse of Peter,* however, blazes a new trail in this regard. As the disciples sit with Jesus on the Mount of Olives, they ask him about the signs of his second coming. Jesus relates his teaching on the end time much as it is found in Matthew 24 but

The *Apocalypse of Peter*

The *Apocalypse of Peter* was composed during the first half of the second century A.D. It circulated widely and gained such popularity that it remained on the fringes of the church's "canon," or list of authoritative texts. The "Muratorian fragment," a late second-century inventory of the church's authoritative scriptures, lists the *Apocalypse of Peter* as a disputed book, while the "Codex Claramontanus" includes it as canonical. By the early fourth century, its status as noncanonical had been established.

goes much further by showing the disciples the fate of those condemned on the Day of Judgment.

On the "Day of God," all people will be gathered before God's judgment seat. The earth will yield up the bodies buried in it, and even animals will give back the human flesh they have devoured, so that all who have ever been alive may stand before God. As earth and heaven are dissolved in flames, the people will pass through a fiery river. Those who are righteous shall pass through unharmed and live with Christ, but the ungodly will be transported into places of endless punishment.

There follows a tour of hell in which Peter sees groups of sinners tormented in ways that make the punishment fit the crime. Those who have slandered God are hung up by their tongues over a lake of fire. Women who made themselves beautiful for the purpose of luring men to adultery are hung up over that flaming mire by their hair, and their partners are suspended by their feet such that their heads are hidden in the boiling swamp. Murderers are tormented by ravenous worms while the victims of their violence look on and praise God for giving them justice. Similarly gruesome punishments await those who have practiced abortion or killed their newborn children, persecutors of the righteous, lying witnesses, those who hoarded their wealth and did not share with the needy, those who lent money and demanded interest, idolaters, apostates, those who failed to care for their parents, those who had sex before marriage, and sorcerers. This part of the vision provides a window into the ethics of the early church. It was an expression of the Christians' criticism of the practices of the society around them, as well as a vehicle for promoting certain values and behaviors within the church (for example, modesty, sexual purity, and sharing with the poor).

Those who are punished cry out to God for mercy, repenting that they did not believe the preaching about God's judgment. Despite their pain, they acknowledge God's justice in punishing them. At this point, there is some disagreement about the contents of the original *Apocalypse*. The righteous are given an opportunity to petition God for the release of whomever they desire. The sinners named by the righteous are baptized and received into paradise. This episode appears in no manuscript of the *Apocalypse of Peter,* but the presence of the story in the second *Sibylline Oracle,* which paraphrases much of the *Apocalypse,* as well as a fragment that seems to come from an earlier version of the *Apocalypse,* suggests that the episode was original. In either case, it shows the concern of early Christians for the problem of discovering

The *Acts of Peter*

The principal source for extrabiblical stories of Peter is the *Acts of Peter,* one of a number of apocryphal "Acts" modeled after the canonical Acts of the Apostles. The *Acts of Peter* was written in Greek before the fourth century A.D. Clement of Alexandria in the late second century and Origen in the early third refer to stories found in these *Acts,* leading some scholars to hold that the document was already available by the last decades of the second century. The section on the martyrdom of Peter also circulated independently. The *Acts of Peter* was translated into Latin during the fourth century, and it is the Latin version that has come down to us.

loved ones
or friends
among the
damned.
How can
one have joy
in heaven if
one's spouse
or child is
in torment?

The transfiguration of Christ

These docu-
ments show how some Christians resolved the
question.

The second part of the *Apocalypse of Peter* pre-
serves an expansion on the story of the transfiguration (Matthew 17:1–8). Jesus took Peter, James, and
John privately up to a mountain, and while he was
praying, his appearance became as radiant as the
sun. Elijah and Moses appeared, conversing with
him about his death and resurrection, and then a
cloud covered the mountain. The voice of God was
heard to say, "This is my beloved Son, in whom I
am well pleased; hear ye him." In the *Apocalypse,*

this episode transpires in part as a response to the disciples' request to see the state of the righteous who have died. Elijah and Moses appear, resplendent with glory, satisfying the disciples' curiosity. Jesus then shows them the regions of heaven where the righteous dwell and how the souls of the righteous are clothed with the garments of shining angels. Peter says here, as he does in the canonical Gospels, "Do you wish for me to make three booths here—one for you, one for Moses, and one for Elijah?" In the canonical accounts, Peter's question is passed over without an answer. Here, however, Jesus replies that Satan has veiled Peter's mind. Jesus opens the disciples' eyes to see the tabernacle made by God for Jesus and all the righteous, and the disciples rejoice.

Blessings in Disguise

The New Testament is full of stories of healings, but the early church also knew of many people who were not healed of their diseases. Was God withholding his favor from these sons and daughters? Why did God not bring physical health to everyone who asked for it? A story about Peter's daughter seems to focus on this troubling question.

While Peter was healing many sick people who had been brought to him, one person asked him why, after healing so many others, he did not heal his own daughter. This girl, though a believer, lay helpless on a mat, completely paralyzed on one side. Peter says that God is certainly able to heal his daughter, and to confirm the faith of those gathered around him, he bids his daughter be healed in the name of Jesus. She immediately rises up and walks across the courtyard to her father. After the people see this and rejoice, Peter bids his daughter to become crippled once more.

Peter tells the bewildered crowd that it is better for his daughter to be afflicted. When she was born, Peter had been told in a vision that his "daughter would harm many if she remained well." Peter had thought nothing of it, but when his daughter was a mere ten years old, a rich man named Ptolemy saw her bathing and desired to have her as his wife. The girl's mother refused, but Ptolemy was so stricken by her beauty that he kidnapped her, intending to fulfill his desire. A short time later, Ptolemy returned with the girl and left her, now struck with paralysis, at Peter's doorstep. Her parents found her, rejoicing that God had thus kept her from being defiled. Peter concludes her story by declaring that "God cares for his people and prepares for them what will be to their greatest advantage, even when it seems God has forsaken them."

A variant of this story is also found in some manuscripts of the *Acts of Peter* and is referred to by Augustine, a highly influential theologian and bishop of the late fourth and early fifth centuries A.D. A peasant farmer has a virgin daughter, and he asks Peter to pray for her. Peter asks God to send her what would be advantageous for her soul, and in response, the girl falls down dead. The farmer, believing this to be a curse and not a divine favor, returns to Peter begging that his daughter's life be restored. Peter complies. A few days later, however, a stranger comes through town and, pretending to be a fellow believer, lodges with the farmer. That night he seduces the girl, and the two ride off together and are never seen again.

The message of both versions is that God provides what is best for his children. Even when afflicted with sickness—or even untimely death—one can be assured that God's providence and good will toward his children have avoided a worse ill. Perhaps readers (ancient and modern) will not be convinced by this explanation, but it represents at least an early and serious attempt by Christians to come to terms with the problem of prayers not being answered in the ways that we would wish.

The Contest Between Simon Peter and Simon the Sorcerer

The canonical Acts of the Apostles introduces the figure of Simon the Sorcerer (or magician, hence the name Simon Magus). He enjoyed a following in Samaria but was himself converted briefly to Christianity by the preaching and wonder-working of Philip the evangelist (Acts 8:9–13). When Peter and John arrived in Samaria to confirm the work of Philip and baptize the converts with the Holy Spirit, Simon offered Peter and John money if they would give him the gift of bestowing the Holy

Spirit upon whomever he touched. Peter vehemently rejected Simon's offer, rebuking him for thinking to buy the power of God with money. The episode ends with Simon asking Peter to pray for him, that none of the evil Peter described might befall him (Acts 8:14–24).

Acts leaves the reader wondering about the fate of Simon Magus, but the early church developed a number of legends about his activity after the Samarian incident. Most of these can be found in the *Acts of Peter* since, throughout his life, Simon Magus remains the nemesis of his namesake, Simon Peter. The contest between these two figures became the expression of the struggle between magic and miracle, sorcery and true religion, the religious charlatan and the devoted pastor. These stories reminded Christians of the victory of their religion over magic and also distinguished their religion as authentic in a world full of impostors and peddlers of pseudospirituality.

The stage is set in the *Acts of Peter* with a brief reference to Paul's ministry in Rome, where he is confirming the faith of many people and bringing new believers to Christ. Paul is instructed by a vision to go to Spain and expand his evangelism efforts to reach the farthest known region to the west (which he also refers to in Romans 15:22–24). After prayers and tearful farewells, Paul and his missionary team leave Rome for points west.

At about the same time, rumors are heard about a certain Simon, a great magician who has been performing wonders in the towns of Italy. Some of the Roman people invite him to come to the capital, and Simon responds, "Tomorrow at the seventh hour you will see me fly over the city gate and appear in Rome." The next day, a shining dust cloud appears on the horizon and then disappears upon reaching the city gate, at which point Simon appears in the midst of the crowd. He is hailed as a god by all witnesses and immediately sets to work undermining the faith of the new Christians. Soon, he has won over all but a few loyal church leaders, who pray to God to send deliverance lest all Paul's work in the city be undone by this charlatan.

God, however, has already called Peter to leave Judea and travel to Rome to combat the

enemy. When Peter disembarks at Puteoli, a port
city south of Rome, he is greeted by Ariston,
a Christian leader whom God has sent from
Rome to wait for Peter and lead him to the city.
Ariston says that the local Christians have lost all
those whom Paul entrusted to their care, but that
his hopes were revived upon seeing Peter. The
Christians scattered about the city hear that Peter
has arrived to expose Simon Magus, and they
gather together to greet Peter. Recalling his own
experience of denying Jesus when tested, and the
mercy he had received when he repented, Peter
tells the believers that it should not come as a sur-
prise that the devil would assault their faith as well.
He uses his own example to encourage those who
have been seduced by Simon to repent and to be
assured of God's mercy.

Peter's first task is to visit a certain Marcellus,
who had been a Christian and a great patron to
the Christian community in Rome. Whenever a
believer had need, Marcellus was quick to provide assistance. Now, however, he is host to Simon
Magus and has repented of wasting his money on

the Christians. Peter arrives at Marcellus's door and announces himself. The gatekeeper informs him that Simon has instructed him to tell Peter, whenever he came calling, that Simon is not at home. Peter, seeing a dog tied to a fence nearby, unties him and tells him to run in among the guests and announce his arrival. When the dog speaks in a human voice, Marcellus and his guests are amazed. Marcellus rushes out to Peter and repents of having followed Simon and withholding his aid from his sisters and brothers. Marcellus recalls how Peter, too, had once lost his faith and doubted (see Matthew 14:22–33) and finds assurance that his own repentance will be accepted as well. We see here why the early church decided not to hide the faults of its first leaders—the failures of a Peter or Thomas did not discredit them but rather helped later generations find comfort and reassurance when they, too, failed and sought restoration.

Marcellus evicts Simon from his house, denouncing him as a deceiver. Having lost face in this match, Simon must try to win it back. He therefore goes to the house where Peter is staying and challenges Peter to come out. Peter instead sends to the door a young mother with her seven-month-old son. The infant speaks with an adult voice and calls Simon an abomination before God and people. The infant further conveys to Simon a word from Jesus: "Be speechless and leave Rome until the next Sabbath." Simon is immediately struck mute, and he leaves the city to lodge in a barn for the remainder of the week.

During this respite, Peter tells the Roman church of his previous encounters with Simon, particularly how he had driven Simon out of Palestine. By means of his magic arts and hypocrisy, Simon had endeared himself to a rich woman named Eubola. When the time was right, Simon used his spells to make himself and two henchmen invisible so that they could steal all the woman's gold and hide it until they could find a safe way to sell it. When Eubola discovered that she had been robbed blind, she had her own servants tortured to elicit a confession. Peter, hearing of this, prayed that the matter would become known. God revealed to him when and where Simon would try to fence the stolen property. Peter told Eubola, as well as the merchant who would be approached the next day, then took four of the woman's strongest servants and hid them in the shop. The next day, Simon's henchmen arrived with some samples of the stolen property. They were taken into custody and forced under torture to reveal the place where the rest was hidden. Simon, waiting outside the city for the deal to be completed, came to the city gate to find out what was taking his partners-in-crime so long. Seeing them hauled off in bonds, he quickly surmised that the truth was out, and he fled Palestine.

The night before the Sabbath, Peter encourages and is encouraged by the believers, and early in the morning he goes to the forum. The Roman people—both the Christians and non-Christians—turn out in droves, hearing of the coming contest between two wonder-workers. Simon, again able to speak, declares the folly of thinking a crucified man is god, and the Romans voice their approval. Peter explains that this was proof God's plan was working—that it was an awesome mystery rather than a cause for mockery. In the end, however, it is a contest of signs, not of speeches, that wins the day. The prefect of Rome, named Agrippa, brings forward a slave and proposes that Simon kill him by his magic, and Peter raise him up. The crowd could decide which was the greater power. Simon whispers a spell into the slave's ear, who immediately falls down dead. At this point, a widow rushes forward to beg Peter's help. Her own son has just died. The men standing around her offer to go with her to her house and bring the corpse to Peter, if she really believes Peter can revive him.

The prefect calls Peter's attention back to the dead slave, challenging him to raise him up. Peter replies that God is not to be tempted but rather worshipped with a sincere heart. Since, however, God is eager to turn the audience from their sins, Peter asks the Lord to revive the slave. Agrippa comes forward at Peter's invitation to take the slave's hand, and when he does, the slave revives and stands upright. The widow's son is then brought into the forum, and in answer to Peter's prayer, God raises him as well. Finally, a senator's wife comes and asks the same gift for her dead son.

Peter now turns the tables on Simon. He proposes that Simon be given a chance to raise a dead person. If he cannot, Peter declares that all should reject him as the deceiver and sorcerer that he is. Simon, who has a trick all ready, calls for Peter's banishment from Rome if he succeeds. The people say they will go further and burn Peter if Simon can deliver. Standing at the head of the corpse, Simon makes the dead man nod his head and open his eyes. At this, the crowds begin gathering wood for Peter's pyre. Peter laughs at their blindness to Simon's trickery. He says, "Let the dead man speak, rise up, untie the linen cloth from around his face and call out to his mother." The crowd offers to burn Simon if Peter can do more than his adversary, but Peter says it would be better to allow Simon to live, so that he might himself repent, since Jesus taught against taking vengeance on one's enemies. With a word, Peter raises the dead man and urges the audience to leave behind their idolatries and worship the God who gives life. The senator's wife and her son become believers, and the church rejoices at Peter's victory over Simon.

In a desperate attempt to regain his reputation and influence in Rome, Simon announces to the people of Rome that he will fly over the city and ascend back to God in heaven. He leaps from an elevated place and begins to fly in plain view of the people. Peter, knowing that Simon's success now would undermine the faith of many, prays to Jesus that Simon would fall from the sky and be injured (but not die from the fall). Simon falls at once to the ground and breaks his leg irreparably. The people demonstrate their disgust with his tricks and leave him disgraced. He departs for Africa and dies following a surgical operation.

The story of Simon Peter and Simon Magus celebrates the victory of Christianity over magic and false gods, and the defeat of heresy and charlatanism by a representative of the apostolic faith. It also illustrates Jesus' teaching on not retaliating.

The Martyrdom of Peter

Peter enjoys considerable success in evangelizing at Rome in the wake of Simon's defeat. Among those whom he converts to the Christian faith

are Agrippina, Nicaria, Euphemia, and Doris—
four concubines of the Roman prefect Agrippa.
Hearing Peter's words about the virtue of chastity,
they determine not to give themselves to Agrippa
anymore for the satisfying of his lusts. Agrippa is
greatly disturbed by this change in their attitude
and has them followed. When they are observed
going by night to the house where Peter is staying, Agrippa concludes that Peter has infected
them with these strange ideas. Peter also wins over
Xanthippe, the wife of a powerful friend of the
emperor, and many others to the virtue of chastity. The Roman men, deprived of their pleasure,
decide to arrest Peter and put him to death as a
troublemaker. Hearing of this plan, Xanthippe
rushes to warn Peter. The believers persuade Peter
to leave Rome so as to preserve his life. As he is
leaving the city, he has a vision of Jesus entering the city. Peter asks him, "Lord, where are you
going?" Jesus replies, "I am going to Rome to be
crucified." Peter realizes that Jesus is calling him
to remain with the believers in Rome and accept
martyrdom—the fulfillment of the word that Jesus

had spoken to Peter shortly after the resurrection (see John 21:18–19).

The death of Peter

Back in Rome, Peter gathers the church to strengthen them in the faith. Four guards interrupt the service, taking Peter into custody. Ignoring the pleas of the Christians, Agrippa sentences Peter to be crucified for the crime of godlessness. At the hill where his cross awaits, Peter requests to be crucified head downward as a witness to the onlookers that the world beholds all things upside down—the good it calls bad, the ugly it calls beautiful. He addresses Jesus in prayer: "You are mother, father, brother, friend, servant, and guardian to me; you are all." Peter expires, thus fulfilling his promise to die for Jesus' sake.

The Apostle Andrew

Biblical Background

here is little said in the synoptic Gospels about the apostle Andrew. He is always overshadowed by his brother Peter and is generally relegated to a subsidiary position when Jesus speaks to the group of 12. Only in the Gospel of John does Andrew gain more attention. He was the first of the apostles chosen and had previously been one of John the Baptist's disciples (John 1:35–40). Andrew brought his brother Peter to Jesus (John 1:41–42), and on at least two occasions he was singled out as the spokesman for the disciples: In one he is mentioned in the story of the feeding of the 5,000 (John 6:8–9), and in the other, Andrew brings word, along with Philip, that Greeks wish to speak with Jesus (John 12:20–22). This lack of information may have led to the composition of the *Acts of Andrew* in the second century. There was a great deal of interest in the lives and deaths of each of Jesus' apostles. Their names and exploits were frequently used to promote a set of beliefs or a theological agenda, most of which were eventually declared heretical.

Gnostic Influences

Andrew, rather than Jesus or church authorities, serves as the source of revelation and the guide to self-realization in the *Acts of Andrew*. He takes it as his task to reveal that the flesh and its needs are a prison for the soul. Only when a person sheds the needs and desires of the body and sees the "new person" within can a full understanding of the word occur. Then, at death, the freed soul can rejoin the divine, merging with the Godhead. Some of these ideas resemble aspects of Gnosticism, a version of early Christianity best known from Egypt that also emphasized the body as a prison for the soul. However, there are not enough exact parallels to suggest that the *Acts of Andrew* was a product of the Gnostic community. Rather, the ideas expressed in it reflect some of the concerns of a mixture of the philosophical movements of the second and third centuries A.D.

The *Acts of Andrew*

The *Acts of Andrew*, written in Greek between A.D. 150 and 200, possibly in Alexandria, Egypt, provides a brief look at Andrew's work as an evangelist and his martyrdom. The *Acts of Andrew* advocates achieving self-realization and a liberation from the constraints of the body. Thus, the author argues for a scanty diet and Christian celibacy, perhaps based on the passage in Matthew 19:12 that says, "there be eunuchs, which have made themselves eunuchs for the kingdom of heaven's sake." There is also a clear sense of dualism in this document, separating the powers of good and evil within the world, calling them the realms of light and darkness.

Andrew's Career as an Evangelist

The third-century *Acts of Thomas* provides one testimony to the tradition that, following Jesus' command to preach the gospel to every corner of the earth (Matthew 28:18–20; Mark 16:15), the apostles divided up the territory among themselves. Andrew's portion was Achaia, the area of Greece south of Macedonia, and most especially the

Peloponnesus. In order to reach this area, with its principal city of Corinth, Andrew travels through western Anatolia, sails on the Aegean Sea, and visits cities in Macedonia and Thessaly. The narrative of his travels to these regions contains a set pattern of events. He is successful in converting whole cities, and he establishes churches through his persuasive preaching and as a result of a series of miracles. In nearly every place, he is faced with some opposition or is forced to exorcize demons who are plaguing individuals or whole communities. No group or demonic being, however, can withstand him. Human opponents are quickly converted to Christianity, and allegiance to other gods evaporates as Andrew casts out demons, raises the dead, and heals the sick and the blind. Andrew always refuses any payment for his services. In this way, the writer differentiates the apostle from magicians and exorcists who made a living from such activity.

One story tells of Andrew's first visit to the city of Patras, at the northern end of the Peloponnesian Peninsula. The proconsul, Lesbius, plans to kill Andrew but instead is converted when the apostle saves him from the attack of two "Ethiopians" (demons). Lesbius becomes a follower of Andrew, and he is instructed in the power of God as he witnesses a series of miraculous events. For instance, as they walk along a beach together, Andrew and Lesbius see a corpse washed up on the shore. Andrew raises the man to life, and they hear his tale of a boatload of men who were on their way to hear Andrew speak when the devil intervened, capsizing their ship and drowning all 39 men aboard. Andrew then calls on God to allow the sea to give up the bodies of the other men. They are washed ashore, and he restores each of them to life.

These acts all parallel the activities of Jesus and the other apostles. Also like Jesus, Andrew has the power to calm a stormy sea (Jesus' instance was depicted in Mark 4:35–39) and, like Moses, his word is defended by God through the occurrence of an earthquake, killing those who denounce him (this incident in Moses' ministry is depicted in Numbers 16:23–33). In this way, the stage is set by the author for Andrew's authoritative speeches that will lay out the path to self-realization.

The Martyrdom of Andrew

Perhaps the most important section of the *Acts of Andrew* deals with his final mission in Patras and his martyrdom. As in previous episodes, Andrew has been successful in converting many people. Among them is Maximilla, the wife of the new proconsul, Aegeates. Andrew had healed her of a fatal disease, and under his instruction, she had chosen to become celibate, no longer submitting to her husband's sexual desires. Andrew also converts Aegeates's brother Stratocles while the proconsul is away. This man comes to faith as a result of Andrew's timely help. A demon has been afflicting Stratocles's favorite slave. Maximilla, fearing for Stratocles's sanity as he beats himself in his grief, calls on Andrew to help. Before the assembled crowd, Andrew prays for God's assistance, using the same prayer to ridicule magicians and "the meddlesome" who have no power to command God's intervention. The demon cries out its submission to Andrew's voice and is banished from all Christian soil, while the slave comes back to himself amid general rejoicing.

Such a public display of power adds to Andrew's reputation and sets the stage for his conversation with Stratocles. Andrew now becomes the "spiritual midwife," birthing Stratocles's understanding and banishing his perplexity and his former beliefs as he had banished the demon from Stratocles's slave. Stratocles becomes Andrew's student, listening to and questioning him night and day, struggling, as Andrew puts it, to be born to faith and fortified in Christ. He thereafter remains always in Andrew's company, along with Maximilla and other disciples.

This idyllic existence, however, could not last. Aegeates returns to Patras and naturally wishes for Maximilla to come and share his bed. She is adamant in her decision to remain chaste, free from "the unclean union with Aegeates." But, knowing her husband cannot be denied forever, she devises a plan to trick him. She sends her maid, Eucleia, each night into Aegeates's bed chamber and in this way his sexual needs are met. Eucleia continues this charade for eight months but then begins to blackmail her mistress, demanding money, clothes, and jewelry. Finally, tiring of her role as Maximilla's surrogate, Eucleia tells the other servants what she has been doing. A dispute results among the servants, some remaining loyal to their mistress and some, under the guidance of the devil, condemning her. Eventually, however, Aegeates gets word of the scandal. He tortures Eucleia to get the full story and then cuts off her hands and feet, leaving her to be eaten by dogs.

Aegeates is out of his mind with rage, but he dares not abuse his wife because she comes from an important family and such a scandal would hurt his career and standing. To make matters worse, one of his slaves tells him of Stratocles's similar infatuation with the teachings of Andrew and his shameful behavior, including appearing in public without servants and doing tasks that are normally performed only by slaves. The slave also tells him that Andrew advocates the "senseless" idea of worshipping only one god. Aegeates, alienated from his wife and brother by this new teaching, decides to eliminate the cause of his troubles.

As they walk through the town, the slave points out Andrew and rushes up, holding him so

Aegeates can question him. Despite the fact that Andrew had once saved Maximilla's life, the apostle has now become the source of great shame to the proconsul. Aegeates therefore imprisons Andrew and boasts to his wife that her "master" is now in his custody. Maximilla regularly visits Andrew in prison despite her husband's attempts to stop her. Andrew encourages her to maintain her resolve to remain "pure," refusing to have intercourse with her husband, even though Aegeates has threatened to torture Andrew if she does not return to his bed.

Convinced by Andrew's words, Maximilla once again refuses Aegeates's demands; as a result Andrew is condemned to die by crucifixion. To make Andrew's suffering last even longer, Aegeates orders that he not be wounded or otherwise weakened while on the cross. Stratocles intervenes, driving away the executioners, but then he and Andrew walk together to the place of execution. Despite his brother's action, Aegeates will not show mercy and orders his executioners to carry out the sentence.

Even before Aegeates's men arrive, Andrew is reconciled to his own death. He reassures Stratocles

and the other disciples that this is for the best.
Andrew bids the executioners to carry out their
work, and they tie him to the cross with ropes.

During the time he is on the cross, Andrew,
smiling, addresses a huge crowd for three days and
nights, saying, "Have you not heard that Jesus is a
man who cannot be punished?" He exhorts them
to see that there is more to existence than this
transitory life. But the mob does not fully understand his words and rushes to Aegeates to force
him to release Andrew.

As the people approach his cross, Andrew speaks
in despair that their love is still for the flesh. He
asks how they can urge him to surrender once
"again to what is transient." Telling Aegeates that
he knows the proconsul has not truly repented
his evil but is only bowing to the cry of the mob,
Andrew refuses to yield to him. When Aegeates
physically attempts to release Andrew from the
cross, the apostle prays for the Lord to take him so
that his departure will be a further sign of encouragement to his followers, and immediately his spirit
departs.

Maximilla takes Andrew's body down from the cross and gives it proper burial. She then spends the remainder of her life in prayer and quiet contemplation of Christ. Aegeates commits suicide in his despair, and Stratocles, refusing to take any of the inheritance he would have received from his brother's estate, renounces all the evils of life, calling Jesus his true friend.

A tale such as this, paralleling as it does in many respects the passion story of Jesus, would have been used to instruct early Christian communities. The persecution Andrew faced would have been familiar to them, and his example of welcoming death as a release from the imprisonment of the body would have encouraged them to face their own martyrdom. However, the excesses of celibacy and the passion expressed for a life "out of the world" for all Christians would have been difficult for the church as well as civil authorities to accept. Thus, the *Acts of Andrew* was declared heretical and inappropriate teaching for the majority of Christians.

John the Apostle

Biblical Background

raditionally known as the "beloved disciple" (see John 13:23–26), John and his brother James were the sons of Zebedee and worked as fishermen on the Sea of Galilee until they were called to follow Jesus (Matthew 10:2). Perhaps because of their youth and impetuosity, they are referred to as the "Sons of Thunder" (Mark 3:17). They were certainly among the most important of the 12 disciples. John is often paired with Peter in the Gospels and in Acts. He witnesses the transfiguration (Matthew 17:1–11), helps Peter prepare the Passover meal that will serve as the "Last Supper" (Luke 22:8), and accompanies Jesus to Gethsemane (Matthew 26:37). His role in the early church seems to be as one of the pillars of the Jerusalem community, although he does travel with Peter into Samaria (Acts 8:14–25). Tradition names him as the author of the Gospel of John, the 3 Epistles of John, and the Book of Revelation.

The Life and Miracles of John

It is most likely John's association with Patmos and the churches addressed in Revelation that is the basis for his activities in the *Acts of John.* Here he travels to many of the cities of Asia Minor, starting with Ephesus, to preach and to perform deeds that will "give glory to the Lord." His first act upon entering the city is to go to the house of a man named Lycomedes, whose wife Cleopatra has been lying paralyzed for seven days. Lycomedes is in such despair over his wife's condition that he dies of grief after showing her to John. Naturally, John is concerned since he has just come to the city and already has a tragedy on his hands. He prays fervently to Christ not to allow his mission to come to an end like this and then calls on Cleopatra to arise in the name of Jesus. She does, but now she must face her husband's death. John tells her to hold fast and have faith in the God who has sent him. He then tells her to call on Lycomedes to arise and "glorify the name of God." Lycomedes is immediately brought back to life, and he and Cleopatra eagerly beg John to stay with them while he is in Ephesus. In this way, John's work begins with a sign of God's power, and he has a local voice raised to support his authority to preach.

There is an assumption in many of the episodes in the *Acts of John* that the apostle must perform miracles in order to break through the stubborn unbelief he faces in Ephesus. One example of this is found in his public healing of a group of elderly women. In order to maximize the effect of this act, John stages his miracle in a theater where the women are brought on stretchers. While they await healing, John takes advantage of his "captive audience" to denounce their greed and their concern for the pleasures of this world. He warns them of the torments in the afterlife faced by those who persist in their pursuit of wealth,

John the apostle

fine food and clothing, adulterous relationships, and power in all its forms. The mass healing is now performed, almost as an afterthought to John's powerful sermon.

Frustrated that all the miracles he has performed seem to have had only minimal effect on the people of Ephesus, John decides to confront them openly at the most sacred spot in the city, the Temple of Artemis (Paul's preaching instigated a similar confrontation with the Ephesians in Acts 19:23–40). This structure was one of the largest temple complexes in the world and was in fact considered one of the Seven Wonders of the Ancient World. John purposely wears an inappropriate garment (black instead of festal white) and, standing in the temple, challenges the power of Artemis, the Greek goddess of the hunt and protectress of young women. He calls on the Ephesians to pray with all their might to Artemis to strike him dead. In this way, John directly poses the question, "Who really is God?"—a point of confrontation that has run throughout the history of Israel and the church (see Judges 6:28–32 and

1 Kings 18:17–40). If Artemis fails to kill him, John says, then he will call on God to put them all to death.

Since these people had seen John raise the dead and do many other miracles, they cry out to him to ask God not to punish them. But John knows only the destruction of Artemis's temple and cult will

The *Acts of John*

Among the apocryphal "Acts" that circulated within the early Christian communities, the *Acts of John* seems to be one of the earliest. Based on its mention by Clement in about A.D. 180, it was most likely authored in Greek (perhaps by Leucius, the reputed author of all five apocryphal *Acts*) in the latter half of the second century. Originally almost as long as the canonical book of Acts, about one third of the *Acts of John* survives in both Greek and Latin versions (which contain some different material). Like the other apocryphal Acts, it emphasizes refraining from sexual activity and consists of a series of episodes depicting John's work as an evangelist in Asia Minor and his ability to perform miracles in the name of Jesus.

cause the Ephesians to be converted. So he prays to God to exorcize the corrupting "demon" (Artemis) who has deceived the people. At once the altar splits apart, and the images of the goddess fall and are shattered while much of the temple building tumbles down, crushing the priest of Artemis beneath a pillar. The frightened Ephesians wildly declare there is but "one God, the God of John!"

Demonstrations of power like this are common enough in the Old Testament. Samson, for example, had pulled down the temple of the Philistine god Dagon upon the heads of the priests and worshippers (Judges 16:23–30). The purpose of the early church, however, was not to kill its enemies, but to convert them. Therefore, John moves quickly to still the fears of the Ephesians. He knows that "conversion by fright" is not a formula for longterm devotion. John treats the new converts gently and agrees to stay in Ephesus to nurture their newfound belief until they can be "weaned" and he can travel on to Smyrna. One sign of the mercy of God that John preaches to the Ephesians is the raising of the priest of Artemis from the dead.

Obedience to the law and the renunciation of desires continue to be John's message throughout the *Acts of John*. These themes are seen in the episode involving a young man who kills his father when the old man rebukes his son for seducing a married woman. John prevents the despondent son from continuing his murder spree against the woman and raises his father from the dead. The son still does not understand John's message, however. Instead he castrates himself, throwing the severed flesh down at the woman's feet to show he can never again fall prey to his sexual desires. But John tells him that it is his inner thoughts and being that must be purified, not the flesh that must be punished.

Occasionally, John uses humor to get his message across. During a journey back to Ephesus, John's company stops for the night, but the apostle cannot sleep because his bed is infested with bugs. John orders them to leave his bed and cluster together quietly, bothering no one else. In the morning the group is amazed to find a great mass of bedbugs waiting patiently in a corner. When John gets up, he tells the bugs they may return to their home, and he tells his friends that the obedience demonstrated by the bugs is a model for irresponsible humans who too often fail to keep God's commands.

The last extended narrative in the *Acts of John* again returns to the theme of chastity. Drusiana, one of John's most devoted followers, was well known to the Christians of Ephesus as a pious woman who had pledged to live with her husband, Andronicus, but to refrain from sexual contact with him. Despite this fact, a young man named Callimachus determines to have her. When Drusiana learns about Callimachus's desire, she feels that she is somehow responsible for his sin and, in despair, she dies.

Callimachus, maddened by his desires and the urging of a demon, bribes one of Andronicus's stewards, Fortunatus, to help him break into her tomb, where he intends to defile the body he could not have in life. As they enter the tomb, Fortunatus is bitten by a snake and dies, and Callimachus, who is stripping Drusiana of her burial garments, is struck down by the power of a "beautiful young man" (either an angel or Jesus—compare this with Matthew 28:2–6).

When John and Andronicus return to the tomb three days after Drusiana's burial, they find these two men sprawled on the floor and are greeted by the angelic being. John brings Callimachus back to life in order to find out what has happened. When he has returned to himself, Callimachus confesses his terrible sins and tells John and Andronicus how the angel had struck him down, saying, "Callimachus, die that you may live!" He realizes that all these things were done so that he would believe in Christ and thus truly live.

John then raises Drusiana so that she may rejoice in Callimachus's conversion and she, in turn, asks that the treacherous steward, Fortunatus, be raised. This act again seems to be an effort on the part of the early church to show that Christians do not wish to take revenge on those who try to deceive or oppress them. However, when Fortunatus comes back to life he is unrepentant and flees from them. They later learn that his snakebite caused his body to swell up and he has again died. His death is therefore his own choice, and John can only say of him, "Devil, you have your son."

The *Acts of John* concludes with John's death and burial. Like Paul, who approached his death as the successful end of a long race run in obedience to God's purpose for his life (as he expresses in 2 Timothy 4:7), John describes himself as one who has "fulfilled his charge." He has two of his followers dig a very deep trench and then stands in it, declaring his thanks to God for keeping him chaste and free of the "union with a woman." Apparently, it had been quite a struggle; John had planned to marry, and God had actually struck him blind for two years to prevent this. In his final words, John calls on God to triumph over all the forces of evil and bring him and all God's children the peace that has been promised them. He then lies down in his grave and gives up his spirit. In this way, the apostle provides a model of a Christian life well-lived and prepared to welcome death when it comes.

Paul, Apostle to the Gentiles

Biblical Background

aul enters the history of the church as a man zealous for the Jewish law, educated as a Pharisee, whose devotion expresses itself in the persecution of the Jewish Christians (Acts 8; Galatians 1:13–14). He met the risen, glorified Jesus in a vision and soon became Christianity's most ardent evangelist. Paul believed that he had been commissioned by God to preach Christ to the gentiles (non-Jews), and so he embarked on a series of missionary journeys throughout Syria, Asia Minor, and Greece. He may even have taken the gospel as far as Spain before his death in or around A.D. 64.

Paul is remembered as a traveling founder of churches and especially as a writer of letters. Fully one-quarter of the New Testament is composed of letters written by or attributed to Paul.

Paul's endurance of hardship and opposition also impressed itself on the church's memory. All of these facets of Paul's career became the basis for apocryphal stories about his work as well as apocryphal texts attributed to Paul's hand.

Paul and Thecla

The figure of Thecla does not appear in the New Testament, but she appears in the *Acts of Paul* as a devoted convert and, eventually, a preacher of the gospel herself. The story opens as Paul, fleeing from Antioch on account of hostility stirred up against him by the synagogue there (Acts 13:44–51), journeys to Iconium. Paul is traveling with Demas and Hermogenes, known as deserters from the faith (mentioned in 2 Timothy 1:15 and 4:10). They are greeted by Onesiphorus (also known from 2 Timothy 1:16 as a loyal supporter of Paul) and taken into his house. There Paul preaches concerning the blessedness of abstinence from all sexual intercourse for the sake of communion with God.

Across the street from Onesiphorus lives a beautiful young woman named Thecla, who is betrothed to Thamyris. She stares out the window, entranced by Paul's teaching on virginity. No matter how loudly her mother, Theoclia, or her fiancé call to her, no one can distract her from Paul's words. Thamyris, concerned not only for himself but for all men who stand to lose their wives to this foreigner's teaching, seeks to know who this man is. Demas and Hermogenes, anxious to overthrow Paul and replace him as teachers themselves, inform Thamyris that Paul teaches that there is no resurrection except for those who remain chaste. They suggest that Thamyris accuse him before the governor as an enemy of the social order, promising to teach him about the true resurrection that already happens for the believer (this is identified as a heretical teaching in 2 Timothy 2:18).

Thamyris hauls Paul before the governor amid shouts of angry men: "Away with the magician who subverts our women!" The governor hears the accusation and Paul's defense and then commits Paul to prison until he can look into the matter further. Thecla comes to visit Paul in prison. Bribing the guards, she is allowed to enter his cell

The *Acts of Paul*

The principal source for early church traditions about Paul is a second-century text called the *Acts of Paul*. Written in Greek, probably in Asia Minor, this collection of "Acts" includes the story of Thecla, a convert to Christianity who came to be venerated as a saint, a rather fragmented narrative of Paul's travels, and an account of the martyrdom of Paul. The sections that purport to preserve Paul's teaching do not depart in major ways from orthodox Christianity, save for the intense promotion of celibacy as a norm for the Christian. Like the *Apocalypse of Peter,* this text was highly regarded by many in the early church as an edifying story, if not as authoritative scripture. When the work came to be exploited by heretics, it quickly fell from favor and use among orthodox believers.

and learns more from him about the good news in Christ. When Thamyris and Theoclia cannot find Thecla anywhere until they discover her in the prison, they accuse Paul of having bewitched her. The governor has Paul whipped and expelled from the city, and Thecla, at her own mother's behest, is sentenced to be burned in the arena as a warning to other women who have been persuaded by Paul. Thecla is led into the theater and bound to the stake but is delivered untouched from the flames by God, who sends a downpour over the arena.

Thecla is released and joins Paul, who has been praying for her deliverance. They travel to Antioch where new trials await Thecla. A rich and powerful citizen of Antioch named Alexander takes an interest in her. When Alexander attempts to take Thecla by force, she rebukes him and humiliates him in public. Disgraced, Alexander brings her before the governor, who condemns her to be killed by the wild beasts in the arena. The women of the city cry out against the unjust verdict, and a relative of the emperor, Tryphaena, takes Thecla into her home until the sentence is to be carried out.

When the time comes, soldiers bring Thecla to the arena and tie her to a fierce lioness. Rather than tear her to pieces, however, the lioness reclines at Thecla's feet. More beasts are let loose, but the lioness kills several of them before being killed herself. Thecla sees a pool of water in the arena and baptizes herself before her impending death. More attempts are made to kill Thecla, but to no avail. Tryphaena faints from the spectacle. The governor and Alexander are terrified at the potential repercussions against their city if a kinswoman of the emperor dies there, so they disband the games and release Thecla. Tryphaena recovers and entertains Thecla for several days in her house, learning about Christ and being instructed in the scriptures.

Thecla leaves Antioch and finds Paul, who commissions her to "teach the word of God." After visiting her estranged mother, she goes to Seleucia and evangelizes there for many years before her natural death.

Galatians 3:28 declares that, in Christ, there is neither Jew nor Greek, neither slave nor free, and no longer male and female. The *Acts of Paul* shows a considerable interest in the last claim. Its emphasis on self-restraint (especially from sexual relations) and its portrayal of women seeks to present a new model for male-female relationships in the early church. The rejection of sexuality gave women a hope for a greater degree of independence (if not equality) and represented a fundamental rejection and critique of the social order itself. The celibate ethic promoted by this story, then, is not merely a rejection of the flesh, but even more directly a rejection of the world.

Stories About Paul's Travels

A number of stories about Paul's travels follow the conclusion of the story of Thecla. Frequently, these expand on brief references that Paul makes to his experiences in his letters but about which no real details are given (such as in 1 Corinthians 15:32).

Paul's authority is brought to bear through the *Acts of Paul* on new heresies that afflicted the second-century church. From the canonical letters (1 and 2 Corinthians), Corinth was known for its susceptibility to new teachings. The *Acts of Paul* invents a scenario in which the Corinthian church is beset by a group of teachers whose doctrine remarkably resembles the message of certain leading Gnostic teachers of the second century. These teachers deny the inspiration of the Hebrew prophets, teach that the God of Israel is not the highest God, and claim that the Christ did not truly become a physical, human being. The Corinthian church leaders write to Paul describing this heresy, and Paul provides a third letter to the Corinthians refuting it point-by-point. The purpose of such a story, of course, is to portray Paul—whose letters were frequently used by Gnostics to support their position—as the staunch opponent of such misinterpretations of his words.

The Death of Paul

As with most apocryphal Acts, this collection ends with an account of the death of the apostle. Paul is traveling from Corinth to Rome by ship, and late at night, he has a vision of Jesus walking toward him on the water. Jesus says to Paul, "I am going to be crucified anew," and instructs him to strengthen the believers in Rome. Like Peter, Paul has a premonition of his own death. This time, however, the hostility of the pagans will engulf the Christian community as a whole.

Luke and Titus—two traveling companions and coworkers of Paul well-known from the New Testament—are waiting for Paul at Rome. The three men rent a barn outside the city and begin to strengthen the believers as well as add many new converts. Patroclus, the emperor's cupbearer (the title for a sort of favorite servant), comes to hear the famous Paul. Unable to get close to Paul because of the crowd of devotees, Patroclus climbs up to a high window and sits there. Satan, attempting to stir up trouble for the believers, pushes Patroclus from the window so that he falls and dies. When he is recognized as the emperor's servant, the believers fear reprisal while others report the incident to the emperor Nero. Paul, however, calms the assembly and, praying for the young man, restores him to life.

As Nero grieves for Patroclus, his servants announce that Patroclus is alive and standing at the door. Nero asks, "Who restored you to life?" Patroclus responds, "Christ Jesus, the king of the ages." Nero is disturbed at the young man's answer. Learning from him that Jesus is to destroy all earthly kingdoms and reign alone, Nero strikes Patroclus's face and asks, "Are you also fighting for that king?" Patroclus affirms that he is, and four of

Nero's trusted courtiers also admit their allegiance
to Jesus. Interpreting this as sedition, Nero orders
them all to be imprisoned and tortured, and he
issues a warrant for the arrest and execution of all
Christians.

Christians are burned to death without trial in
such numbers that non-Christian Romans beg the
emperor to stop before he destroys the strength
of Rome. Nero agrees, turning his attention now
to Paul, his final victim. While imprisoned, Paul
preaches the gospel to two Roman officers, Longus
and Cestus. Because they have not been fully
convinced before Paul's death, the apostle instructs
them to go to his grave early the next morning.
The order for Paul's execution comes down from
Nero, and Paul is beheaded. Later that same day, as
Nero confers with his officers, Paul appears to the
assembly and indicts Nero for his unjust slaughter
of the virtuous Christians, promising great punishments for him in the future. Terrified, Nero
commands that the remaining Christian prisoners
should be released. The next morning, Longus and
Cestus go to Paul's gravesite, where they find Titus

Additional Documents About Paul

Several other traditions about Paul circulated in the early church. A series of letters appeared in the fourth century, alleging to preserve the *Correspondence of Paul and Seneca*. Seneca was a Stoic philosopher whose ethical teaching was greatly admired in the church. His moral teaching seemed almost "Christian" to many, and so a legend developed that he was in fact converted to Christianity by reading the letters of Paul and through corresponding with him. Seneca and Paul were contemporaries, but there is no indication that they met or that Seneca converted to Christianity. Rather, these apocryphal letters sought to give Seneca's ethical instruction a Christian pedigree.

The *Apocalypse of Paul* was written near A.D. 388. In 2 Corinthians 12, Paul refers to a visionary experience in which he was taken "up to the third heaven . . . into paradise" and shown things he was not permitted to speak about. In this lengthy narrative, the author of the *Apocalypse of Paul* describes what Paul had seen in this otherworldly journey. Like the *Apocalypse of Peter,* this vision of the afterlife served to reinforce the moral teaching of the Christian church by portraying vividly the consequences of virtues and vices.

and Luke praying. As they draw nearer, however, they also see Paul praying with them, unseen to Titus and Luke. Longus and Cestus reassure Luke and Titus that they have come not to harm Paul's friends but rather to be baptized by them.

This account of the execution of the apostle Paul and other believers in Rome highlights the political dimension of Christianity. Religion was not strictly a private matter in the first-century world, where loyalty to the empire and to one's fellow citizens was often expressed by means of participation in emperor worship and the cults of traditional Greek or Roman gods. The declaration that a crucified Jew would return to judge the kingdoms of the world and reign as king over all could easily be understood, and punished, as treason. Nevertheless, the willingness of many believers to die for this Jesus, and the remembrance of the courage of leaders like Paul, made many pagans come to rest their hope in the kingdom of God rather than in the goddess Roma.